The New York Times

CROSSWORDS FOR YOUR COFFEE BREAK

Edited by
Will Shortz

ST. MARTIN'S GRIFFIN ☙ NEW YORK

The New York Times

CROSSWORDS FOR YOUR COFFEE BREAK

WHOPPER

by Patrick Jordan

ACROSS

1. Greta who never actually said "I vant to be alone"
6. Howled like a hound
11. This instant
14. Extraterrestrial
15. Popeye's sweetie
16. Gardner of Tinseltown
17. Restaurant gadabout
19. Blend
20. Pesky insects
21. Christians' ___ Creed
23. Surfeit
26. Made fractions
27. Fold, as paper
28. One-dimensional
29. Forebodings
30. Zippy flavors
31. Uneaten morsel
34. Chaney Jr. and Sr.
35. Hats' stats
36. Fencing blade
37. Dehydrated
38. Star-to-be
39. Montreal baseballers
40. Held responsible (for)
42. "Accept the situation!"
43. Bing Crosby or Rudy Vallee, e.g.
45. Penny-pinching
46. Coarse-toothed tool
47. Stun gun
48. Egyptian snake
49. Dazzling performer
54. Victory sign
55. Cassettes
56. Speak
57. Be mistaken
58. Bewildered
59. Former Russian sovereigns

DOWN

1. Gangster's gun
2. Chicken ___ king
3. Barbecued treat
4. Antwerp residents
5. Unity
6. Pirates' plunder
7. Zurich's peaks
8. Sharp bark
9. Periods just past sunset
10. Infers
11. Egotistical conversationalist
12. Sheeplike
13. Like shiny floors
18. Despise
22. Spy org.
23. Chide, as a child
24. Knight's protection
25. Adolescent rock fan
26. Mel's on "Alice," for one
28. Lolled
30. Track official
32. Try to stop a squeak again
33. Snappish
35. To an extent
36. Quotes in book reviews
38. Rummy variation
39. Depose gradually and politely
41. ___ Angeles
42. Pugilist's weapon
43. Desire deeply
44. Part of a stairway
45. Term of address in "Roots"
47. Overly precious, to a Briton
50. Photo ___ (pol's news events)
51. Local educ. support group
52. Always, in verse
53. Southern Pacific and others: Abbr.

THINK: PINK

by Peter Gordon

ACROSS

1. Comedian Mort
5. Small dent on a fender
9. Picket line crossers
14. Margarine
15. Cookie with a creme center
16. Diamond weight
17. Vegas card game
19. Dress style
20. Bullfight bull
21. Marx who wrote "Das Kapital"
23. Sault ___ Marie
24. Flue residue
26. Suffix meaning "approximately"
28. Lucille Ball, e.g.
30. Where the Eiffel Tower is
32. Feed bag contents
34. Distinctive doctrines
35. Fast-growing community
37. Housebroken animal
39. Savior
42. Till bill
43. Yearned (for)
46. Weapon in a silo, for short
49. Found's partner
51. Muse of love poetry
52. Organized absenteeism of police officers
54. Turf
56. "The ___ in the Hat" (rhyming Seuss book)
57. Writer Fleming
58. Greek letter
60. Ark builder
62. Greek letter
64. Stew vegetable
68. Build
69. Forearm bone
70. Indonesian island
71. Appears
72. Christmas carol
73. Settled, as on a perch

DOWN

1. Cry loudly
2. Start (and end) of the Three Musketeers' motto
3. London airport
4. Kooky
5. Martial arts schools
6. Rhymester Gershwin
7. Giraffe's prominent feature
8. Racing vehicle
9. Burn with hot water
10. Baseball's Ripken
11. Gets up
12. Small chicken
13. Spirited horses
18. Actress ___ Scott Thomas
22. Set a top in motion again
24. Police radio alert, briefly
25. ___ Paulo, Brazil
27. Inventor Elias
29. ___ and yon (in many places)
31. "Hi, honey!" follower
33. Egyptian symbols of life
36. Verdi opera based on a Shakespeare play
38. Incited
40. Kooky
41. Of the windpipe
44. Greek letter
45. "i" piece
46. Long-billed wading birds
47. Actress Bloom
48. Jumper's cord
50. Exceed in firepower
53. Decrees
55. Basketball's Shaquille
59. Woody Guthrie's son
61. Rhyme scheme for Mr. Eban?
63. 1900, on a cornerstone
65. Opposite WSW
66. Rhyming boxing champ
67. Annual basketball event: Abbr.

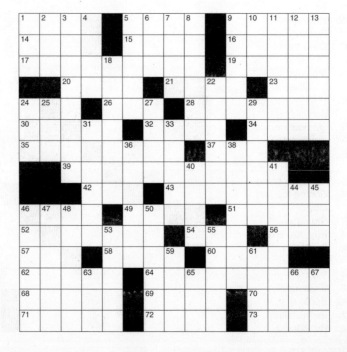

SO HAPPY TOGETHER

by Stephanie Spadaccini

ACROSS

1. The ex-Mrs. Bono
5. Money owed
9. Pharmacy items
14. Composer Schifrin
15. Anatomical passage
16. Like "The Twilight Zone" episodes
17. Actress Lena
18. This ___ of tears (life)
19. Do watercolors
20. Secondhand store
23. Showed respect for the national anthem
24. Sister of Osiris
25. Mr. O.
28. Cinematographer Nykvist
30. Arthurian sorcerer
32. Harvest goddess
35. Pass, as laws
38. Verdi heroine
39. John Glenn's Mercury spacecraft
43. Type assortment
44. Card catalogue entry after "Author"
45. Before, in verse
46. Overage
49. Boat propellers
51. Loaf with seeds
52. ___ to the throne (prince, e.g.)
55. Laid, as a bathroom floor
58. Member of the police
61. Without ___ in the world
64. Prefix with China
65. Nat King or Natalie
66. ___ says (tots' game)

67. ___-do-well
68. Popular fashion magazine
69. Israeli port
70. Microbe
71. Do one of the three R's

DOWN

1. Drain problem
2. Angels' headgear
3. Ness of "The Untouchables"
4. Musical movements
5. Stockholder's income
6. Catchall abbr.
7. Attorney Melvin
8. Lock of hair
9. Remove from office
10. Harvest

11. Spoon-bender Geller
12. Rummy game
13. Matched items
21. Made on a loom
22. That guy
25. Kicking's partner
26. Contract add-on
27. Nonsensical
29. Political cartoonist Thomas
31. "Norma ___"
32. Bidder's amount
33. Stockholder's vote
34. Subsequently
36. Letter before psi
37. Maverick Yugoslav leader
40. High season, on the Riviera
41. Railroad station area

42. Printing flourish
47. Singer Easton
48. Ocean
50. Deli machine
53. Cake decoration
54. "Walk Away ___" (1966 hit)
56. French school
57. Singer Reese
58. Univ. teacher
59. German border river
60. Marsh stalk
61. Cigarette waste
62. K.G.B.'s cold war foe
63. "___ the only one?"

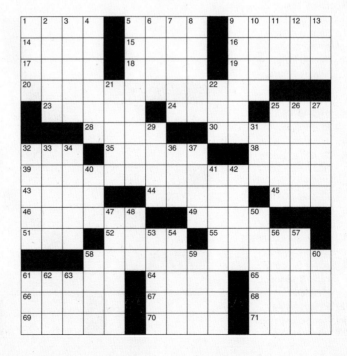

HOLD IT

by Hugh Davis

ACROSS

1. Mad dog worry
5. Spy ___ Hari
9. Aware, with "in"
14. Water color
15. Valentine's Day matchmaker
16. Hawaiian veranda
17. "Brilliant idea!"
20. Ice Follies venue
21. Maid's cloth
22. Veteran
26. Pennilessness
30. ___ Strait (Russia-Alaska separator)
31. Confront
32. Wide shoe specification
33. Police operation
34. Knob
35. Nos. on a road map
36. Classic Bill Clinton phrase
39. Giant Mel et al.
40. Jazzy Fitzgerald
41. Remove, as a knot
43. Award for a knight: Abbr.
44. Neighbor of Vietnam
45. Like some kisses and bases
46. Novelist Hesse
48. Sentimentalists, maybe
49. Superlative ending
50. Subject of psychoanalysis
51. 1962 Cary Grant/Doris Day movie
59. Actor Bruce of radio's "Sherlock Holmes"
60. Chess finale
61. "God's Little ___"
62. Lachrymose
63. Hardly any
64. Rural carriage

DOWN

1. Sheep's sound
2. Stats for eggheads
3. Egyptian boy king
4. Barber's obstruction
5. Cooking up
6. Change, as a motion
7. Swiped
8. Comic dog's bark
9. Split asunder
10. Jessica of 1976's "King Kong"
11. Prefix with cycle
12. ___ de vie
13. Insult, in slang
18. Pumpkin-colored
19. Food seller
22. Out-of-date: Abbr.
23. Last Beatles album
24. Gadabout
25. Jazzman "Fatha"
26. "The Taming of the Shrew" locale
27. Change names
28. Even smaller
29. "You bet!"
31. April ___ Day
34. Parachute material
35. Babbled
37. Shanty
38. Delay
39. Aah's partner
42. U.S.N. officer
44. Summing-up word
45. Flew alone
47. Olympic race unit
48. Conductor Zubin
50. "Get outta here!"
51. Explosive inits.
52. Hasten
53. ___ Khan
54. Thurman of "Pulp Fiction"
55. Mothers
56. "___ bin ein Berliner"
57. Gun enthusiast's grp.
58. Codebreaker's discovery

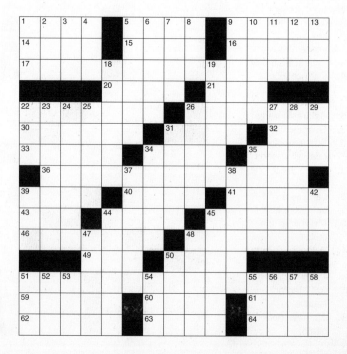

FOR THE FEATHER BRAINS

by Fred Piscop

ACROSS

1. Meal at boot camp
5. Sell tickets illegally
10. Sam the ___ of 60's pop
14. "Beetle Bailey" dog
15. It's a no-no
16. Car with a meter
17. Lose one's nerve
19. Israeli guns
20. Tennis great Rosewall
21. Bohemian
22. "Gunsmoke" star James
24. Vulgar one
26. Tyke
27. 70's–80's Yankee pitching ace
34. Imus's medium
37. Goods
38. "Blue" bird
39. Abba of Israel
40. Opera headliners
41. Stupor
42. ___'easter
43. Sheets, pillowcases, etc.
44. Put on the payroll
45. Old instrument of punishment
48. "Who ___ you?"
49. Sounded, as a bell
53. Prestige
56. Villa d'___
58. Actress Gardner
59. Major league brothers' name
60. Quaint dance
63. "___ the Mood for Love"
64. Actress Samantha
65. Microwave, slangily
66. Grandmother, affectionately
67. Immunizations
68. ___ off (plenty mad)

DOWN

1. Treats cynically
2. Lucy's best friend
3. Children's author R. L. ___
4. League: Abbr.
5. Audiophile's setup
6. Quitter's word
7. "It's ___!" (proud parents' phrase)
8. Singer Rawls
9. Shepherd's pie ingredients
10. Publicity seekers' acts
11. Smog
12. X or Y, on a graph
13. Ole ___
18. Nonmusician's musical instrument
23. Flagmaker Betsy
25. Opposed to, in the backwoods
28. Playground equipment
29. Overhangs
30. Research money
31. Not quite shut
32. Stare, as at a crystal ball
33. Checked out
34. Pull apart
35. "___ Ben Adhem"
36. Jeanne ___ (French saint)
40. Eating alcoves
41. Pickle flavoring
43. Italian money
44. Nonsense
46. Hawaiian medicine man
47. Frolicking animals
50. Lash ___ of old westerns
51. Call forth
52. Went out with
53. Old Testament murderer
54. ___ mater
55. Nickel or copper, but not tin
56. Therefore
57. Three-player card game
61. "Yecch!"
62. Blaster's need

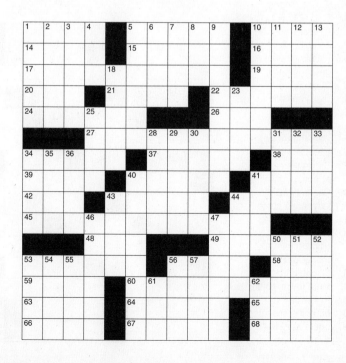

ABOVE AND BEYOND

by Eileen Lexau

ACROSS

1. Prop up
6. Goddess pictured in Egyptian tombs
10. Fraud
14. Old autos
15. Short letter
16. Patriot Nathan
17. Feeling really good
20. Get-out-of-jail money
21. Hors d'oeuvre spread
22. Song for Aida
23. Chomped down
24. "___ cost to you!"
25. Novelist Waugh
27. Batter's goal
29. Frigid
30. "Turandot" slave girl
31. Moon-landing vehicle
32. ___ de Triomphe
33. "I ___ Grow Up" ("Peter Pan" song)
34. Heads of state get-together
38. "It can't be!"
39. Be in session
40. Nothing
41. Peas' holder
42. Pennies: Abbr.
43. Creeks
47. Storm warnings at sea
49. Clinton's #2
50. Wrestler's place
51. Site for a swing
52. Rikki-tikki-___ (Kipling mongoose)
53. Capable of
54. Little that's visible
57. Poker call
58. Mending site
59. Louis XIV, 1643–1715
60. Hawaii's state bird
61. Remove from office
62. Dunne of "I Remember Mama"

DOWN

1. Thick-trunked tropical tree
2. Italian soprano Scotto
3. Clarinetist Shaw and others
4. Refrigerate
5. One of Kreskin's claims
6. Wee one
7. ___ voce (almost in a whisper)
8. Spillane's "___ Jury"
9. Visualize
10. Beach
11. Set of bells
12. Relieving
13. Club ___
18. They expect the best
19. Undulating
24. "Um, excuse me"
25. Like a three-dollar bill
26. Cashew, e.g.
28. "Tickle me" doll
29. Anger
32. Quantity: Abbr.
33. Sly trick
34. Cable channel
35. Support
36. "___ the season . . ."
37. Radial, e.g.
38. Photo ___ (media events)
42. Musical sign
43. Bygone Russian group
44. Electrical unit
45. Female attendant
46. Cheap cigar
48. Sierra ___
49. Scottish Celts
52. 10 C-notes
53. Opposite of unter, in German
54. Can's composition
55. Notwithstanding that, briefly
56. Biblical priest

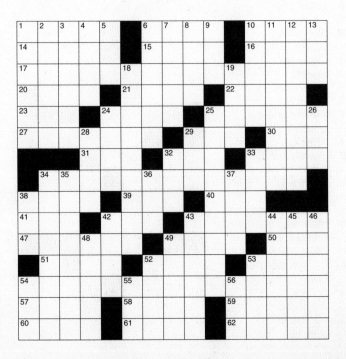

LOCATION IS EVERYTHING

by Gregory E. Paul

ACROSS

1. Civil disorder
5. Urban haze
9. Diners
14. Workers' protection org.
15. Variety of fine cotton
16. Hold dear
17. Tizzy
18. The New Yorker cartoonist Peter
19. Chateau-Thierry's river
20. "Petticoat Junction" setting
23. Lyricist Rice
24. Granola grain
25. Copyists
27. Trim, as a tree
32. Arp's art
33. Military address: Abbr.
34. Fishing line
36. The "S" in WASP
39. State north of Ind.
41. Adventures
43. Battle of Normandy objective
44. Big news exclusive
46. Reading lights
48. Ames and Asner
49. Pub orders
51. Practice
53. Edmonton's province
56. Everything
57. Random number generator
58. "Father Knows Best" setting
64. Texas site to remember
66. Have __ good authority
67. Sewing case
68. Georgia city, home of Mercer University
69. Color of linen
70. Final Four inits.
71. Pronunciation symbol
72. Make-believe
73. Eschew

DOWN

1. __ ha-Shanah
2. "Money __ object!"
3. Louisville's river
4. Dragon, perhaps
5. Big Ten team from East Lansing
6. Nuclear missile, briefly
7. Prefix meaning 56-Across
8. London lockups
9. Kodaks, e.g.
10. Nabokov novel
11. "The Phil Silvers Show" setting
12. Sgt. Bilko
13. Looks like
21. Prominent rabbit features
22. Digital readout, for short
26. Mrs. McKinley and others
27. Beavers' constructions
28. Kind of proportions
29. "I Dream of Jeannie" setting
30. Marsh duck
31. "Pomp and Circumstance" composer
35. Shiny fabric
37. Auto pioneer Ransom
38. Victory margin, at times
40. Tunnel
42. Moss for potting plants
45. __ non grata
47. Prefix with starter
50. Nascar sponsor
52. Little green men
53. Revolutionary leader Samuel
54. Light purple
55. Pisces's follower
59. Scratch it!
60. Nick and __ Charles
61. Make an aquatint
62. Hilo feast
63. Primatologist Fossey
65. Cut the grass

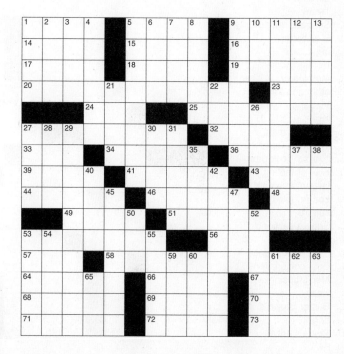

LAST ROUNDUP

by Thomas W. Schier

ACROSS

1. Org. that safeguards pets
5. Prefix with port
9. Liability's opposite
14. Songwriter Gus
15. Plow animals
16. Marvy
17. "Yikes!"
18. Actress Hayworth
19. Mississippi ___
20. Lead singer with Dawn
23. Opposite of 42-Across
24. Alphabet trio
25. Reduced fare
26. ___ la Douce
28. What "hemi-" means
30. Odd
33. Popular record label
36. Cosmetician Elizabeth
37. Treaty
40. Seabees' motto
42. B or better
43. Impassive
45. Horses' home
47. Morning or afternoon travel
49. Vlad the Impaler, e.g.
53. Stallion's mate
54. Water, in Cadiz
56. "Do Ya" rock grp.
57. Kind of testing, in law enforcement
59. Los Angeles suburb
62. Sonata section
64. Mrs. Chaplin
65. Jazz performance
66. Dual conjunction
67. Men's business wear
68. Buster Brown's dog
69. Pirate's prize
70. Nobelist Wiesel
71. TV's "___ Three Lives"

DOWN

1. Artist's rendering
2. Chinese temple
3. Estee Lauder rival
4. Rooney of "60 Minutes"
5. Frightful
6. Banish
7. Free to attack
8. ___ instant (quickly)
9. Neighbor of Spain
10. Go out with
11. 60's–70's A's third baseman
12. Ending with Henri
13. Wart-covered creature
21. Stench
22. Morse code click
27. Baseball owner Schott et al.
29. Bluebeard's last wife
30. Actress Thompson
31. Storm or Tracker, in the auto world
32. Finis
34. Postpaid encl.
35. It's a blast
37. Utilities watchdog grp.
38. From ___ Z
39. "Dirty Dozen" marauder
41. Inflexible
44. Superficial, as a look
46. Emulate Pisa's tower
48. Tetley product
50. Cosmetics applicator
51. Senior years
52. Blew a horn
54. Run ___ of (violate)
55. Bottled spirits?
57. Cheerless
58. Banned act
60. Bloodhound's sensor
61. ___ spumante
63. Complete an "i"

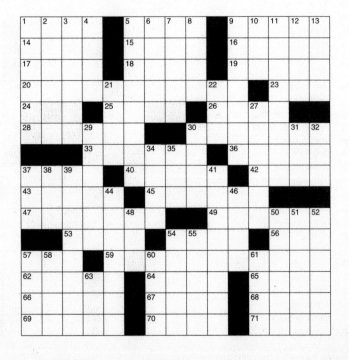

THIS MEANS WAR

by Gene Newman

ACROSS

1. Musicians' copyright grp.
6. King with a golden touch
11. Business fraud monitoring agcy.
14. TV exec Arledge
15. "Be ___ . . ."
16. Spanish gold
17. Grant vs. Bragg, Nov. 1863
19. Tease
20. Sandwich choice
21. Parkers feed it downtown
23. ___-do-well
24. Black Sea port
25. Wakeful watches
28. Bush aide John
30. Neighborhood
31. Idiot
32. Chinese food additive
35. On, as a lamp
36. For fun
38. Place for a hole in a sock
39. Winter clock setting in Vt.
40. Union branch
41. Coal stratum
42. "Old ___" (1957 Disney film)
44. Lines of cliffs
46. Slugged
48. Salon job
49. Perth ___, N.J.
50. Unlike Mr. Spock of "Star Trek"
55. Brock or Costello
56. Rosecrans vs. Bragg, Sept. 1863
58. Continent north of Afr.
59. Eagle's nest
60. Listlessness
61. It follows a dot in many on-line addresses
62. Not our
63. Syria's Hafez al-___

DOWN

1. It may have fallen on a foot
2. Manhattan locale
3. Jacket
4. Cather novel "My ___"
5. Small sea bird
6. Millionaire's home
7. Elvis Presley, in the 50's and 60's
8. "I ___ it!" (cry of success)
9. H.S. math
10. Patrick Ewing specialty
11. Anderson vs. Beauregard, Apr. 1861
12. Attempts
13. Striking snake
18. Good blackjack holdings
22. Poet's dusk
24. ___ about (lawyer's phrase)
25. Caesar's farewell
26. Spring bloom
27. Meade vs. Lee, July 1863
28. Kind of energy or flare
29. ___ Mountains (edge of Asia)
31. Riot queller
33. Ivory, e.g.
34. Onyxes and opals
36. Night prowler
37. Auctioneer's last word
41. Pago Pago residents
43. D.D.E.'s command
44. ___ poor example
45. Sevastopol locale
46. Ancient: Prefix
47. Love affair
48. Fireplace rod
50. Dublin's land
51. 1102, in dates
52. Women in habits
53. Tijuana water
54. Deposited
57. Sneaky laugh sound

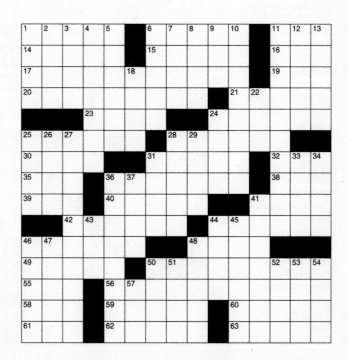

MIXED EMOTIONS

by Shannon Burns

ACROSS

1. Deep sleeps
6. Abbr. before an alias
9. Fragrant oil
14. ___-garde
15. Steal from
16. Push roughly
17. A Roosevelt
18. Afflicted with strabismus
20. Traffic tangle
21. The first "H" of H.H.S.
22. Quilting event
23. Cautious
24. Open a bit
28. Garbage barge
30. Come down
31. Clinton's #2
32. Sigma follower
33. Blue birds
34. Grown-ups
36. Snares
38. Shooting marble
39. Bill settlers
40. Coating metal
41. "Are we there ___?"
42. They're exchanged at weddings
43. Building block company
44. Goofs up
45. Of ships: Abbr.
46. Second-year student, for short
47. Not a beginner
48. Get down from a horse
50. Thesaurus compiler
53. Show with Richie and the Fonz
56. Dancer Astaire
57. Banish
58. Gun grp.
59. Brusque
60. "For ___ sake!"
61. Opposite NNE
62. Industrial city of Germany

DOWN

1. Long-running Broadway show
2. Turkey roaster
3. Paul Reiser/Helen Hunt series
4. President Jackson or Johnson
5. Do, as hair
6. Architectural frames
7. Ones with Seoul custody?
8. "All ___!" (conductor's cry)
9. Helper: Abbr.
10. Where Dutch royals live
11. Plaything
12. "___ Maria"
13. Like Time's border
19. Crafty
25. Pirate flags
26. More pretentious
27. Bowling alley buttons
28. Enter
29. The Great White North
30. Swimmer's regimen
33. Place for pickles
34. ___ time (never)
35. Nov. follower
37. Fasten papers again
38. Visited tourist places
40. Gentle breezes
43. "___ Run" (1976 sci-fi film)
44. Wears away
46. Rock singer Vicious
47. Chatter
49. Caustic solutions
51. Otherwise
52. Adolescent
53. Wise, man
54. Chop
55. Orchestra's location

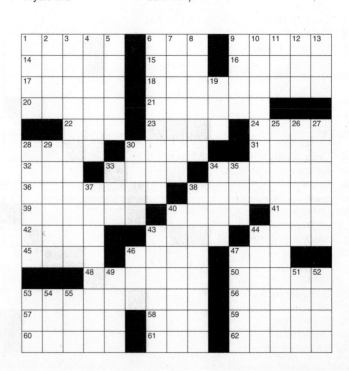

SLEEP ON IT

by Peter Gordon

ACROSS

1. Throat-clearing sound
5. Fencing weapon
10. Actress Rowlands
14. Exploding star
15. Singer Page
16. Fairy tale's second word
17. St. Paul and Minneapolis
19. Require
20. Comedians Bob and Chris
21. In a wise manner
23. Lawyer's charge
24. "Gee!"
25. Sweatshirt part, perhaps
27. Flush beater
32. Writer Bellow and others
33. Place for a pimento
34. Not the swiftest horse
35. Posterior
36. "Death Be Not Proud" poet
37. Opera star
38. Dog breeder's org.
39. Imply
40. Doled (out)
41. Leaders of hives
43. Like some tea
44. Praise
45. Santa __, Calif.
46. Refuse to acknowledge responsibility for
49. Post-marathon feeling
54. Quickly, in memos
55. Southern crop, from an economic standpoint
57. Writer Grey
58. Writer Zola
59. Humorist Bombeck
60. Got a good look at
61. Saw socially
62. Profound

DOWN

1. Pot starter
2. Loud laugh
3. More than devilish
4. Part of a car's exhaust system
5. Malice
6. Light bulb unit
7. Elevator inventor
8. Road map abbr.
9. Liquefy
10. Very enthusiastic
11. Fencing weapon
12. Christmas song
13. Raggedy Ann's friend
18. Some college students
22. Tennis great Arthur
24. Quick flashes of light
25. 17-syllable poem
26. Precious metal unit of weight
27. Paid, as a bill
28. Arm bones
29. Come together
30. Backed up on disk
31. "Holy cow!"
32. The N.B.A.'s O'Neal, familiarly
36. Exposed as false
37. Poured wine into another container
39. Chew
40. Actor Sal
42. Ran for one's wife?
45. Moved like a shooting star
46. Stun
47. British exclamation
48. Having all one's marbles
49. Tizzy
50. Leer at
51. To be, in Bordeaux
52. Not all
53. Jacket fastener
56. The Monkees' "___ Believer"

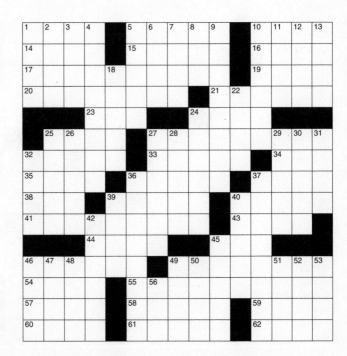

BAG OF BONES

by Gregory E. Paul

ACROSS

1. "Othello" villain
5. Flat-topped hills
10. Colonel Mustard's game
14. Eschew
15. Some of the Pennsylvania Dutch
16. Feed bag contents
17. Filly's mother
18. "Truly!"
19. Takes advantage of
20. Jalopy
23. Poker starter
24. "Roses ___ red . . ."
25. Like a lot
28. Fawn's mother
31. Necklace units
35. Come about
37. Department of Justice div.
39. Tiny
40. Autumn 1940 aerial war
44. Prior to, poetically
45. Mao ___-tung
46. Tenor Caruso
47. Council of Trent, e.g.
50. Flower holder
52. Spud
53. Lawyer's thing
55. Texas Western, today: Abbr.
57. Mule, e.g.
63. Kind of purse
64. Sidestep
65. Norse Zeus
67. Five-time Wimbledon champ, 1976–80
68. Vintner Ernest or Julio
69. Girl-watch or boy-watch
70. ___-Ball (arcade game)
71. Church officer
72. Marsh plant

DOWN

1. Doctrine: Suffix
2. Captain obsessed
3. Maven
4. Like some diamonds, sizewise
5. "Luncheon on the Grass" painter Edouard
6. Chewed the scenery
7. Fodder storage site
8. "___ I cared!"
9. Yemen, once
10. Grand ___ Dam
11. Word before laugh or straw
12. Salt Lake City students
13. Feminine suffix
21. Toll
22. Regalia item
25. French clerics
26. Hon
27. Time after time
29. Bid
30. Retrocede
32. Lie in store for
33. Winter windshield setting
34. Sir, in Seville
36. What may be followed by improved service?
38. Dander
41. Buckeyes' sch.
42. The "I" in ICBM
43. Cause of an unexpected fall
48. Jellybean flavor
49. ___ Plaines, Ill.
51. Marriageable
54. Old Wells Fargo transport
56. Elizabeth I was the last one
57. Library unit
58. Dublin's land
59. Elliptical
60. Quit, in poker
61. Winning margin
62. Longest river in the world
63. "60 Minutes" network
66. TV's "___ and Stacey"

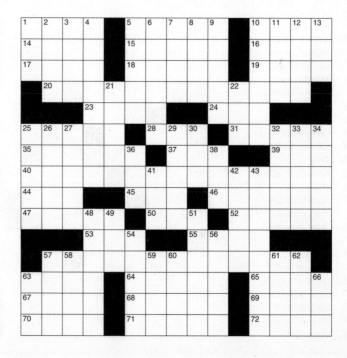

FLAG DOWN

by Mark Elliot Skolsky

ACROSS

1. Tarzan's love
5. Bungle
10. Tickled
14. Johnny Cash's "___ Named Sue"
15. Before the due date
16. Singer McEntire
17. Formative Picasso phase
19. Terrible czar
20. It picks up readings
21. Hustler's tool, maybe
23. Religious council
25. Actor Davis
26. Assail
30. Football Hall-of-Famer Merlin
32. Newspaper publisher Adolph
33. Year, south of the border
34. Wouldn't proceed
39. Center of a 1994 chase
42. Apollo 13 commander
43. Holds
44. Tennis champ Bjorn
45. Cleaner/disinfectant brand
47. Connection
48. Octagon or oval
52. One of "The Honeymooners"
54. "Carnival of Venice" violinist
56. Tough
61. Jai ___
62. Sophie Tucker was the "last"
64. Opposite of ja
65. Writer Asimov
66. General's command
67. "Auld Lang ___"
68. Tailor
69. Bean counters, for short.

DOWN

1. Quick punches
2. Up to the task
3. Verb preceder
4. Potato parts
5. Drunken
6. Paddle
7. July 14, in France
8. Sun blockers
9. F.D.R.'s ___ Park
10. Southern breakfast dish
11. Popular pants since 1850
12. Old-style calculators
13. "Thanks, Gerhard"
18. Hitching ___
22. Sub's "ears"
24. Taboo
26. New Year's Day game
27. 22-Down reply
28. Hood's knife
29. Villa d'___
31. Trails off
33. Be ___ in the ointment
35. Earring locale
36. Fort ___ (gold depository site)
37. Stocking shade
38. Labradors and Yorkshires
40. Comedienne DeGeneres
41. Flamboyant Surrealist
46. Most mentally sound
47. Not masc. or fem.
48. Crosses over
49. Alex who wrote "Roots"
50. One more time
51. "Common Sense" pamphleteer
53. "Time in a Bottle" singer Jim
55. Pupil locale
57. Detroit financing co.
58. "The World According to ___"
59. Austen heroine
60. From nine to five, in the classifieds
63. Kubrick's "2001" mainframe

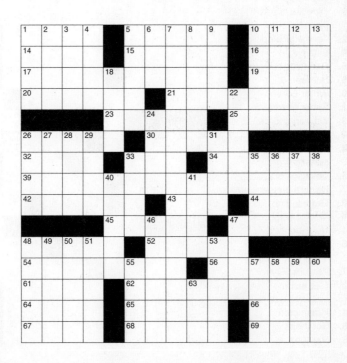

MEDICINE MEN

by Gregory E. Paul

ACROSS

1. "Quite contrary" nursery rhyme girl
5. Sudden outpouring
10. June 6, 1944
14. Pinza of "South Pacific"
15. "Here ___ trouble!"
16. Straight line
17. Chest organ
18. Make amends (for)
19. Goat's-milk cheese
20. 60's TV medical drama
22. Detective Lord ___ Wimsey
23. Guinness suffix
24. Shooting stars
26. World Wildlife Fund's symbol
30. "The Hairy Ape" playwright
32. Gets educated
34. Finale
35. Deep cut
39. Saharan
40. Writer Bret
42. Butter alternative
43. ___ contendere (court plea)
44. Kind of "vu" in a classified
45. Colossus of ___
47. Hardy's partner
50. Get used (to)
51. Medicine injector
54. Neighbor of Syr.
56. Enough to sink one's teeth into
57. Pasternak hero
63. "___ just me or . . . ?"
64. Indian corn
65. Not theirs
66. Rat (on)

67. TV's "Kate & ___"
68. Romance lang.
69. In ___ (actually)
70. She had "the face that launched a thousand ships"
71. Fuddy-duddy

DOWN

1. Blend
2. Cote d'___
3. N.H.L. venue
4. Cartoon bear
5. Oodles
6. Latke ingredient
7. Cupid
8. Rent-controlled building, maybe
9. WNW's opposite
10. British rock group since the mid-70's
11. Because of
12. Take up, as a hem
13. Sophomore and junior, e.g.
21. Low-fat
22. ___ Club (onetime TV group)
25. Downy duck
26. Scheme
27. Prefix with dynamic
28. It gets hit on the head
29. 1967 Rex Harrison film role
31. Moxie
33. Shoulder motion
36. Actor Alan
37. Trickle
38. Party thrower
41. Wiry dog
46. Spy Mata ___

48. Unspecified one
49. Tin ___
51. Wallop
52. O.K.'s
53. Train tracks
55. Luster
58. Streamlet
59. Empty
60. Garage occupant
61. Alum
62. Sonja Henie's birthplace
64. ___-jongg

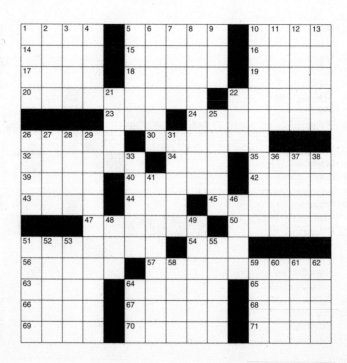

CLEAN HOUSE

by Patrick Jordan

ACROSS

1. "If I ___ the World" (pop hit)
6. Boutique
10. Kind of carpet
14. Glue
15. Carbonated canful
16. Scarlett's plantation
17. Run to the altar
18. Brother of Cain
19. N.M. neighbor
20. Accounting principle, for short
21. Comic strip witch
23. ___ Steamer (early auto)
25. Land west of Britain
26. Brain wave reading: Abbr.
27. Track records?
29. Sine ___ non
32. Journalist Alexander
35. Isn't on the street?
36. Phoenix fivesome
37. Defeat decisively
40. "Ball!" callers
41. Scolds ceaselessly
42. Birchbark boat
43. Toothpaste type
44. Days of long ago
45. Inclined (to)
46. Feldman role in "Young Frankenstein"
48. Mill in 1848 news
52. Seal tightly, as a coffee can
56. Cleveland's lake
57. Memorable periods
58. Tiny bit
59. Area of corporate investment, briefly
60. 1996 Broadway hit
61. Walked (on)
62. Popular watch brand
63. Plumb loco
64. Slangy assents
65. German industrial city

DOWN

1. Movie units
2. Illuminated from below
3. Bath sponge: Var.
4. Square numbers?
5. Hair coloring
6. Hair-raising
7. Traveling tramp
8. Bogus butter
9. Tree with fan-shaped leaves
10. Flight of steps
11. Clown
12. Dry, as a desert
13. Disputed Mideast strip
21. Entreat
22. Towel inscription
24. One of Jacob's wives
27. Unwelcome water on a ship
28. Seth's son
30. Next-to-last word of the golden rule
31. Tennis's Arthur
32. Self-satisfied
33. "Fourth base"
34. Resume submitter
35. From a distance
36. Specialized police units
38. Outrageousness
39. Sales slip: Abbr.
44. Last word of the golden rule
45. Northern diving bird
47. Bursts of wind
48. Gazillions
49. Sea eagles
50. Chain of hills
51. Alternative to a convertible
52. Sink or swim, e.g.
53. Vicinity
54. Skin opening
55. On the peak of
59. ___ v. Wade (landmark decision)

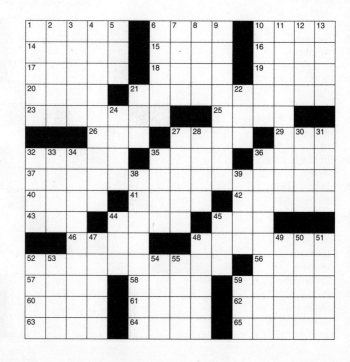

MUSICAL?

by Gregory E. Paul

ACROSS

1. Neanderthal's weapon
5. Basketballer
10. Tramp
14. Sharpen, as a razor
15. Dateless
16. Finished
17. Touch up, as text
18. Repeated Chris O'Donnell movie role
19. Org. expanding into Eastern Europe
20. Healthy
23. Toward the stern
24. September bloom
28. Mother that can't be fooled
32. Much of kindergarten
35. Sports venue
36. Woeful word
37. The first X of X-X-X
38. Spotless
42. No longer working: Abbr.
43. Parts of bytes
44. "Frasier" character
45. Weaken
48. Ulcer cause, in popular belief
49. Emergency room supply
50. Cosmonauts' space station
51. Taut
59. Certain boxing blow
62. Send, as payment
63. Seldom seen
64. Mitch Miller's instrument
65. "Goodnight" girl of song
66. The dark side
67. Still sleeping
68. Copier powder
69. A.F.C. division

DOWN

1. Worker with an apron
2. New Jersey city south of Paramus
3. Army outfit
4. VHS alternative
5. Chianti container
6. Skyward
7. Mongolian desert
8. Camelot lady
9. Split
10. "I'm telling you the truth!"
11. Lab eggs
12. Craps action
13. Treasure of the Sierra Madre
21. See-through wrap
22. Minstrel's song
25. Y.A. of the Giants
26. Novelist Zola and others
27. Alcove
28. Mother-of-pearls
29. Longtime "What's My Line" panelist
30. Wobble
31. Spanish article
32. Batter's position
33. Statutes
34. Baseball bat wood
36. "___ was in the beginning . . ."
39. Lawyers' org.
40. Prefix with venous
41. Madam's mate
46. Like a wagon trail
47. George Marshall's alma mater, briefly
48. Nun
50. Down East
52. Stick-to-itiveness
53. Submarine sandwich
54. Feds
55. Attracted
56. Strong thumbs-up review
57. "Mila 18" novelist
58. Liquefy, as ice cream
59. Mauna ___
60. Decline
61. Antagonist

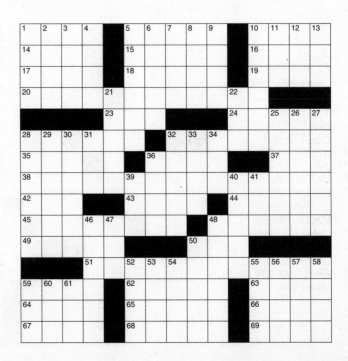

TOM-FOOLERY

by Daniel Halfen

ACROSS

1. Webster's, e.g.: Abbr.
5. Ones easily fooled
9. Afflictions
14. Jacob's twin
15. "Not guilty," e.g.
16. Dwelling place
17. Green shot
18. Bibliography, basically
19. Cheek cosmetic
20. Parts of lbs.
21. Diagonally
23. Put safely to bed, as a child
25. Peewee
26. Steal cattle
29. Actor Nielsen of "Airplane!"
33. Practices in the ring
35. Be jubilant
37. Octopus's defense
38. Cheryl of "Charlie's Angels"
39. Louvers
40. Lavish affection (on)
41. Lubricate
42. Taxonomic divisions
43. Clerics' confab
44. 2 or 3, maybe, on the Richter scale
46. Macbeth and others
48. ___ Normandes (Channel Islands)
50. Tidbit
53. Dry bouquet item
58. ___ and cry
59. Poppy product
60. Stead
61. 1995 porcine Oscar nominee
62. Not so good
63. Muscat's land
64. Rainless
65. Lip-curling smile
66. Telegraphed
67. Caddie supplies

DOWN

1. Train stop
2. Trooper on the highway
3. Children's string game
4. Syllable of reproach
5. Aid for a fracture
6. Dismounted
7. Buzzy one
8. Mythical goat/man
9. British sir
10. Cuts short, as a space flight
11. Verb accompanier
12. Advantage
13. Prophet
21. Smooch
22. Picks out
24. Northern Iraqi
27. "The Windsor Beauties" painter
28. Praise
30. Biggest portion
31. Absorbed by
32. Scraped (out)
33. Coin hole
34. Twosome
36. Great Salt Lake site
39. Nagger
40. One turning color?
42. Nylon, for one
43. Skiers' wish
45. Treat badly
47. Quantity
49. Missile pits
51. Jazz pianist Blake
52. City north of Sheffield
53. Some camp denizens, for short
54. "Once ___ a time . . ."
55. Beget
56. Margarita fruit
57. Like Jack Sprat's diet
61. Dracula, at times

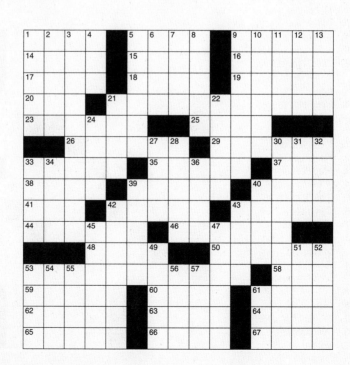

AROUND THESE PARTS

by Joel D. Lafargue

18

ACROSS

1. Cleopatra's love ___ Antony
5. Dressed like Dracula
10. Frozen waffle brand
14. Controversial orchard spray
15. Open-mouthed
16. ___ of Arc
17. Coffee, slangily
18. Half note
19. Roof's edge
20. Post-Derby interview spot
23. Camel rival
24. L-1011, e.g.
25. Sign after Aquarius
28. Land bordered by the Mekong
30. Beanie
33. With 54-Across, a Revolutionary hero
34. Algebra or trig
35. Scarlett's estate
36. 1965 Gary Lewis and the Playboys hit
39. Four-star review
40. Andy of the comics
41. Otherworldly
42. Neighbor of Wyo.
43. Reps.' opponents
44. Parts of acts
45. The "L" of L.A.
46. Dullsville
47. Flabbergast
53. Freq. quotation attribution
54. See 33-Across
55. Mormon state
57. ___-deaf
58. For rent
59. Recipe directive
60. Washstand vessel

61. Mild oath
62. Many millennia

DOWN

1. Capt.'s better
2. "There oughta be ___!"
3. Sitarist Shankar
4. Engine housing
5. Relief carvings
6. "If I Had ___ Like You" (1925 hit)
7. Opposites of a 39-Across
8. Many a Cecil B. De Mille film
9. Large bottle
10. Tape deck button
11. Hockey score
12. Contributed
13. "My ___ and Only"
21. Immensely

22. Legal matter
25. ___ dish (lab item)
26. "___ to Be You"
27. Hindu Trinity member
28. Reading lights
29. Sitting on
30. Stone mound
31. 70's sitcom
32. Capitol Hill gofers
34. Sir's partner
35. Branch office?
37. Emulate Oksana Baiul
38. Stick-on
43. Bespectacled dwarf
44. Viewpoints
45. Hardly a partygoer
46. Animal variety
47. Comprehend

48. ___ of the above
49. Whip
50. Stewpot
51. Director Preminger
52. Excedrin target
53. Had a hero?
56. Action film "48 ___"

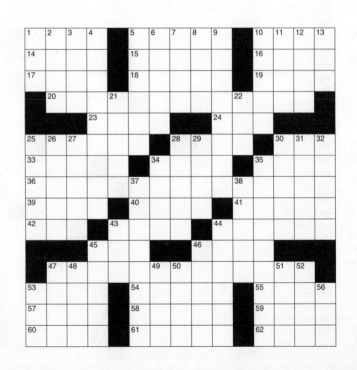

ANIMAL CRACKERS

by Randall J. Hartman

ACROSS

1. Clinch, as a victory
6. R.B.I., e.g.
10. Keats, for one
14. Got out of bed
15. "Sock it ___!"
16. Fairy tale's first word
17. Super Bowl I champs
20. Slalom curve
21. New Jersey five
22. Kind of monkey
23. Anklebones
24. June 6, 1944
25. Yummy items
29. TV's "L.A. ___"
32. Waters: Lat.
33. "Xanadu" rock grp.
34. Remove from a manuscript
35. Sound of a cat or engine
36. Like Jack Benny, famously
38. More than a vogue
39. Pecan and pumpkin
40. Sought election
41. Had money in the bank
42. Sault ___ Marie
43. Football defensemen
46. It gets slapped around a lot
47. Skin cream ingredient
48. Book after Song of Solomon
51. Z ___ zebra
52. Hawaiian dish
55. On-line menaces
58. Nobelist Wiesel
59. Old Dodge
60. Artist's support
61. Bambi and others

62. When a factory whistle blows
63. Mink wrap

DOWN

1. Wise
2. Blows it
3. Trials and tribulations
4. Take advantage of
5. Mark Twain, for one
6. Kind of electricity
7. 1992 Robin Williams movie
8. Sound stage equipment
9. Sign of sorrow
10. Hoosegow
11. Billfold bills
12. Light beige
13. "___ of the D'Urbervilles"

18. Dracula player Lugosi
19. Princely abbr.
23. Ivan and Nicholas
24. Boxer Oscar ___ Hoya
25. Northern Scandinavians
26. Phrase of resignation
27. Blender setting
28. Nancy Drew's creator
29. "Scram!"
30. Creator of the Ragged Dick books
31. Garden intruders
34. Circumnavigator Sir Francis
36. "Jurassic Park" novelist
37. Length of yarn

41. Candle brackets
43. Hawaiian do
44. Smash, as a windshield
45. Inter ___
46. Flutist
48. Clinched, as a victory
49. ___ survivor
50. Parisian lady friend
51. Florence's river
52. Baja buck
53. Pitcher Hershiser
54. Bermuda, e.g.
56. Comic Philips
57. Kit ___ Club

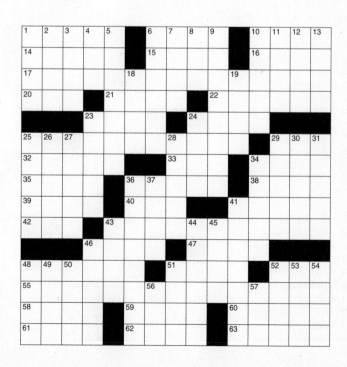

MARK TIME

by Gregory E. Paul

ACROSS

1. Destine to disaster
5. Pepper's partner
9. Fix (in)
14. ___ Major
15. Pop singer Brickell
16. TV's "Kate & ___"
17. Word with land or critical
18. Score before 15
19. One who raises a stink?
20. Famous Wall Street panic
23. Reverse of WNW
24. De-squeaked
25. Travel far and wide
27. Make war
30. Modern refrigerators do it automatically
33. Prefix with cycle
34. Actor Davis
37. Field enclosure
38. Marksman of Swiss legend
40. Exodus mountain
42. Mideast's Gulf of ___
43. Spud
45. Skin: Suffix
47. Yucatan year
48. Well-read
50. Kind of piano
52. Deftness
53. Faint, as through ecstasy
55. Sit-ups firm these
57. 1971 Steve McQueen film
62. Officer-to-be
64. Fountain drink
65. Overhang
66. Mannerism
67. Lackawanna's partner in railroading
68. Pavarotti piece
69. Final approval
70. Poetic contraction
71. Old Fords

DOWN

1. Slow-witted
2. Like some vaccines
3. Bones
4. Army's mule, e.g.
5. Concerned only with others
6. Idolize
7. Enraged
8. Ready to be hit, as a golf ball
9. Popular oven cleaner
10. Jan. 15 initials
11. 1957 Fats Domino hit
12. One, to Hans
13. Astronaut Slayton
21. Narc's unit
22. "All the Things You ___"
26. Side squared, for a square
27. Montana city
28. Lend ___ (listen)
29. "Voices Carry" pop group
30. Honeybunch
31. Happening place
32. Voice above baritone
35. Team
36. Suffix with elephant
39. Helen's mother, in Greek myth
41. Charlatan
44. Italian rice dish
46. Major League brothers' name
49. Half a score
51. Temper, as metal
53. Trap
54. Poet Elinor
55. ___ of the Apostles
56. Theda of Hollywood
58. "You said it, brother!"
59. Bull's-eye hitter
60. Ardent
61. Yes votes
63. Frozen Wasser

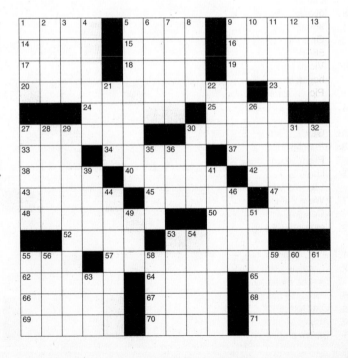

FUNNY BUSINESS

by Robert Goldberg

ACROSS

1. One of the Three B's of classical music
5. Milkshake conduit
10. Church recess
14. Field measure
15. Nile capital
16. Close, as an envelope
17. "Horse Feathers" stars
20. Put in stitches
21. Orders to plow horses
22. Eagle's nest
23. Pencil's innards
24. New York nine
26. Eastern philosophy
29. Scandalous gossip
30. Getty product
33. Broadcasts
34. Larger than quarto
35. 9-to-5 grind
36. Genre of 17-and 56-Across
40. Vietnamese holiday
41. Picnic places
42. First murder victim
43. Gawk at
44. Prevaricates
45. Placid
47. Hairless
48. Stocking flaws
49. West Indies, e.g.
52. Connect, as girders
53. Where: Lat.
56. "The Outlaws Is Coming" stars
60. Jacket
61. Hot coal
62. Escape battle
63. "___ springs eternal"
64. Like many attics
65. Classify, as blood

DOWN

1. Cave dwellers
2. Feel sore
3. Rowing sport
4. Skirt's edge
5. Reaction on a roller coaster
6. Burdened
7. Barbecued dish slathered with sauce
8. Flightboard abbr.
9. Court
10. Cigar residue
11. Equal
12. Indian dress
13. "What ___ is new?"
18. Long, long time
19. Skin art
23. Speech problem
24. Dairy products
25. Newsman Sevareid
26. Flavor
27. Choreographer Alvin
28. Declaim
29. Links with a space station
30. Diving bird
31. Poet W. H. ___
32. Flair
34. Out of a job
37. Quite a display
38. Mermaid feature
39. Pathfinder's locale
45. Torrid
46. Inner: Prefix
47. Divine Miss M
48. Stopwatch button
49. Compulsive desire
50. "Begone!"
51. Quantum ___
52. Insect snares
53. Hideous
54. Pager sound
55. Expression of understanding
57. Claret color
58. Ostrich kin
59. Frequently

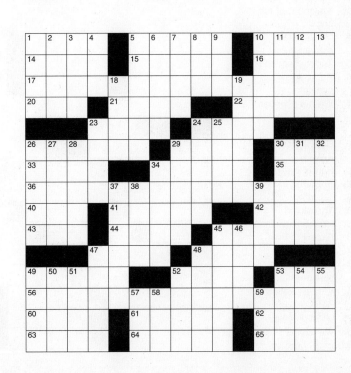

ALL WET

by Stephanie Spadaccini

ACROSS

1. Amo, ___, amat (Latin practice)
5. College prep exam
9. Thin and bony
14. Singer-actress Lorna
15. "Picnic" playwright
16. Daddy Warbucks's little girl
17. Prefix with phobia
18. Years and years
19. Get together
20. Demonstrate affection like a plumber?
23. Saharalike
24. ___ Khan (ex of Rita Hayworth)
25. Place to park a car
29. French cheese
31. Krazy ___ of the comics
34. "Tiny" Albee character
35. Tugboat sound
36. Prefix with dynamic
37. What a plumber says to noisy kids?
40. Days before big events
41. Bands' bookings
42. Preferred invitees
43. TV room
44. Therefore
45. Vertebral columns
46. Exploit
47. Gloomy guy
48. Declines, as a plumber?
56. Where Leonardo was born
57. Oklahoma city
58. Atmosphere
59. Part of the pelvis
60. Sicilian blower
61. Ribald
62. "E pluribus unum," e.g.
63. Like a busybody
64. Dummies' replies

DOWN

1. "Woe is me!"
2. Lots of
3. 60's hairdo
4. Put away
5. South Dakota's capital
6. Very white
7. Lambs: Lat.
8. Experiment
9. Charles de ___
10. Bother
11. Purdue, e.g.: Abbr.
12. Evening, informally
13. Golfer's gadget
21. Made a border
22. Port-au-Prince's land
25. Stared openly
26. Breathing
27. Get ready to be picked
28. One-spots
29. Beatnik's drum
30. Paddles
31. Enter, as computer data
32. Got up
33. Praises loudly
35. Branch offshoot
36. "___ Wanna Do" (Sheryl Crow hit)
38. Monsters
39. Run out, as a subscription
44. Igloo dweller
45. Half a weekend
46. Not abridged
47. Procures
48. Where fodder is stored
49. Monogram unit: Abbr.
50. High schooler
51. "I'm ___ you!"
52. Voting district
53. Meal on Maui
54. Mezz. alternative
55. Paths
56. Energy

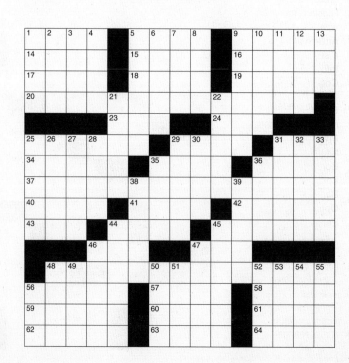

SUITABLE FOR FLYING

by Gregory E. Paul

ACROSS

1. Separate, as flour or ashes
5. Forum language
10. Paul Bunyan's ox
14. Doughnut's middle
15. Primitive calculators
16. Military no-show
17. Bit of physics
18. "Dear friend!"
19. Door sound
20. Overjoyed
23. April 15 initials
24. Paper purchases
28. Egg-rolling time
32. Reddish-brown horse
35. Copper, e.g.
36. Greeting at sea
37. Hush-hush govt. group
38. Highly pleased with oneself
42. Afternoon hour on a sundial
43. Info
44. Country singer Crystal
45. Garbage-marauding critters
48. Present and future, e.g.
49. Borden's cow
50. Forbid
51. Bonkers
59. Opposite of all
62. Perch
63. "___ to leap tall buildings . . ."
64. Skunk's defense
65. TV duo Kate and ___
66. Carbonated drink
67. Overhaul
68. Bread maker
69. Trial balloon

DOWN

1. Mideast ruler of years past
2. Small amount
3. Dud
4. Office fill-in
5. Actress Hedy
6. Vast chasm
7. Novelist Janowitz
8. Suffix with poet
9. One of Columbus's ships
10. Two-pointer
11. Cobbler's tool
12. Feathered stole
13. Shade tree
21. Submit
22. Four Monopoly properties: Abbr.
25. Pesters
26. Biceps, e.g.
27. Belmont ___
28. Sovereign's domain
29. Antenna
30. Zeno and others
31. Fraternity "T"
32. Cowboy's wear
33. Aspiration
34. Hurricane's center
36. "Unto us ___ is given"
39. Fuss
40. 60's rocket stage
41. Soup container
46. Roman orator
47. Poet's preposition
48. Sampler
50. Count of jazz
52. Lebanese, e.g.
53. Defender of Dreyfus
54. Egg part
55. Wear well
56. Mitch Miller's instrument
57. The "O" in R.E.O.
58. Peachy-keen
59. Neither's partner
60. "___ to a Nightingale"
61. Doze (off)

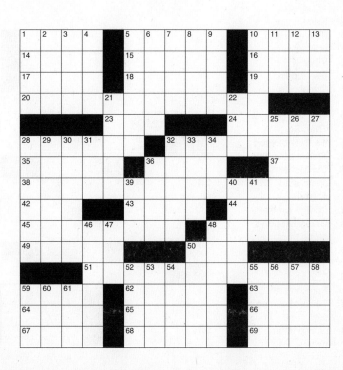

THAT FIGURES

by Randy Sowell

ACROSS

1. Response to an insult
5. Tibetan monk
9. Snack chip
14. Prefix with dynamic
15. Pastoral poem
16. "Not you ___!"
17. Expressway access
18. Big bag
19. Saltine brand
20. Attractions near the Nile
23. Doorway
24. Elderly
25. Orthodontist's org.
28. Sights around road repairs
33. "Quiet!"
36. Fishing equipment
37. ___ Ababa
38. Rural outing
41. Fine gold and enamelware
43. Viper
44. Swiss peak
45. Question's opposite: Abbr.
46. 1, 8, 27, 64, etc.
51. That: Sp.
52. It's 21% oxygen
53. Stallone title role
57. Components of some auto engines
62. Screen symbols
64. Grand Dragon's group
65. Barely passing grades
66. "___ and Punishment"
67. Table of contents, e.g.
68. ___ spumante (wine)
69. 18 on a golf course
70. Canyon effect
71. Distribute, with "out"

DOWN

1. "Beetle Bailey" character
2. Gain knowledge
3. Medieval helmet
4. Warhol's genre
5. Have trouble with esses
6. "An apple ___ . . ."
7. Sherlock Holmes's brother
8. Acid neutralizer
9. "Schindler's List" villain
10. Elderly
11. Prophetess of Greek myth
12. Strike
13. "Put ___ Happy Face"
21. Scandinavian war god
22. 1600, to Cato
26. Condescend
27. Biblical beasts of burden
29. Common conjunction
30. Finder's ___
31. Taxi
32. "___ to the West Wind"
33. Mold
34. Devil's domain
35. Swift watercraft
39. Third man in the ring
40. Anger
41. Winter bug
42. Police alert, for short
44. Kind of paint
47. Convertible or coupe, e.g.
48. Amuse
49. White-tailed eagle
50. Iraq's Hussein
54. Reagan Attorney General Edwin
55. Royals great George
56. Actor Davis
58. "This one's ___"
59. Applies
60. Whip
61. "What's gotten ___ you?"
62. German "I"
63. ___-Magnon

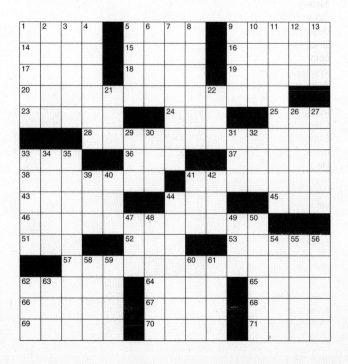

STAR-CROSSED LOVERS

by Barbara Campitelli

ACROSS

1. The Bee Gees brothers
6. Subside
9. Big hit, in Variety slang
14. Journalist ___ Rogers St. Johns
15. Inlet
16. Zhou ___
17. Classic film duo
20. Andean animals
21. Entrance
22. Villa d'___
23. Old card game
26. Film ___
27. Sirs' counterparts
32. "Catcher in the Rye" author
37. "My Three Sons" son
38. Classic film duo
40. The "A" in RAM
41. Vanquished
42. Nearby things
43. Go over 212 degrees
44. Bird on a U.S. coin
45. Weaving machine
49. Actor Emilio
54. Old-time actress Ina
56. Classic film duo
59. Stradivari's mentor
60. Help
61. Itsy-bitsy
62. Without face value, as stock
63. Numbered hwy.
64. Swashbuckling Flynn

DOWN

1. Bit of Gothic architecture
2. False gods
3. Fathered, biblical-style
4. Hold responsible
5. F.D.R.'s mother
6. Cenozoic, e.g.
7. Coal container
8. Nag, nag, nag
9. Vanquished
10. A single time
11. Imperfection
12. F.D.R.'s pooch
13. Unctuous
18. Former Presidential aspirant Paul
19. Tollbooth part
24. Popular brand of faucet
25. Spaniel, for one
27. Look dejected
28. With 49-Down, former Israeli statesman
29. Border
30. Bog
31. Fedex, e.g.
32. Suffix with thermo-
33. Part of the foot
34. Shoestring
35. Boardwalk coolers
36. Where bulls and bears run: Abbr.
37. Mirror
39. Greeting to Hitler
43. Charity event
44. Poet's period after dusk
45. Cake part
46. Long-spouted can
47. University of Maine town
48. Streep of "Out of Africa"
49. See 28-Down
50. Japanese wrestling
51. Golf hazard
52. Jazz singer ___ James
53. To see, in Marseille
55. Overdue
57. Small point to criticize
58. J. F. K.'s predecessor

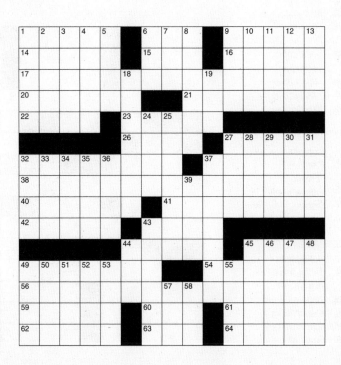

DO AS I SAY

by Gregory E. Paul

ACROSS

1. "___ Network" (1980's comedy series)
5. False god
9. Phillips head item
14. ___ vera
15. Austen's Woodhouse
16. Mild cigar
17. Unload, as stock
18. Ruler's length
19. Hammerin' Hank
20. "Just one gosh-darn minute!"
23. Rebel (against)
24. Vim
25. Part of the Dept. of Trans.
28. Like a taxi
31. Scrooge's cry
34. The "A" in James A. Garfield
36. Tire fill
37. Inter ___
38. "Be polite!"
42. Actress McClurg
43. Handyman's vehicle
44. Detail map
45. Poor grade
46. Preschooler's auto accessory
49. Opposite NNW
50. Hockey's Bobby
51. Farm unit
53. "Hush!"
60. Stocking stuffer
61. Singer Guthrie
62. Russia's Itar-___ news agency
63. Musical eightsome
64. Peter the Great, e.g.
65. Nights before
66. Beach spot
67. Chumps
68. Start all over

DOWN

1. Window frame
2. Nile queen, informally
3. Tunnel fee
4. South African expanse
5. "Age ___ beauty"
6. Add up (to)
7. Love, to Livy
8. Builder's backing
9. With knees knocking
10. Purse part
11. Scarce
12. February 14 figure
13. Triumphed
21. Scrumptious
22. "La Bohème," e.g.
25. Widely known
26. Put up with
27. Golfer with an "army"
29. Takes home, as salary
30. Basketball backboard attachment
31. Hallow
32. Buenos ___
33. Waste maker
35. Fruit drink
37. Landers with advice
39. Egg maker
40. Former Mideast inits.
41. Explosive, informally
46. Devise
47. Part of a cold-weather cap
48. The "A" in S.A.G.
50. Playful water animal
52. "Come in!"
53. "Brandenburg Concertos" composer
54. "___ each life some . . ."
55. Horse's mouthful
56. Celestial bear
57. Donated
58. Not new
59. Sinclair rival
60. "Send help!"

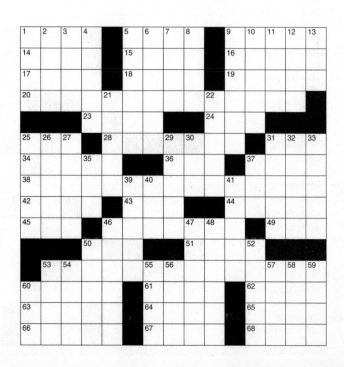

HOP TO IT

by Peter Gordon

ACROSS
1. Frosts, as a cake
5. Give off an odor
10. "Iliad" or "Aeneid," e.g.
14. Trig ratio
15. No-no
16. Warrior princess of TV
17. Declare with confidence
18. TV-top antenna
20. 1996 Michael Crichton novel
22. Confidential matter
23. Skeleton's place?
24. Broad valleys
26. "So there!"
28. Sprinted
29. Dripping
32. Town square
36. Genesis garden
38. Jazzy talk
39. Nutty thought
42. Tennis great Lendl
43. Humor columnist Bombeck
44. Harbingers
45. Physicist's workplace
46. Mensa members have high ones
47. ___-fi (book genre)
49. Rockne of Notre Dame
51. Once a year
56. Set of advantages
59. Generosity
61. Beginners' skiing area
63. Price
64. Actor Estrada
65. Uses a Smith-Corona
66. Competed

67. There are 435 in Cong.
68. Sesames, e.g.
69. Makes mistakes

DOWN
1. Stern that worked with a bow
2. Kind of engineer or service
3. Month after diciembre
4. Feudal workers
5. Layers
6. Sir's counterpart
7. Receded
8. Arcing shot
9. Perry White was her boss
10. Company V.I.P.'s
11. Prickly ___
12. Legal memo starter
13. It's made of plaster of paris
19. Selective Service registrant, agewise
21. Post-op period
25. Sports venues
27. Cosmopolitan publisher
29. Broad
30. Like left-hand page numbers
31. Lipton products
32. Comedian Hartman
33. Volcano output
34. United ___ Emirates
35. Kind of Buddhist
37. Not too intelligent
38. "Huckleberry Finn" character
40. Bands take them

41. Performing
46. Annual Memorial Day event
48. Gentle stroke
49. Difficulties to be worked out
50. Run off to the chapel
52. Chutzpah
53. Pan Am rival, formerly
54. Daisylike bloom
55. Yorkshire city
56. "Deutschland ___ Alles"
57. Undiluted
58. Scissors cut
60. Mimicked
62. Soapmaker's solution

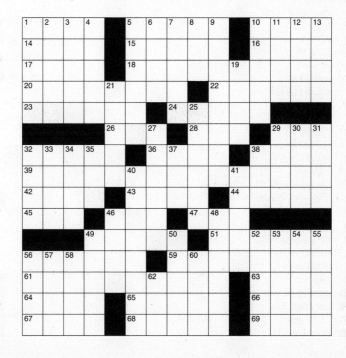

EVERYTHING OLD IS NEW AGAIN

by Mark Gottlieb

ACROSS

1. "Gee whillikers!"
5. Like a good lounge chair
10. Go steady with
14. Follow, as orders
15. ". . . like a big pizza pie, that's ___" (old song lyric)
16. Russian river or mountain
17. "St. Elmo's Fire" actor Rob
18. Sinks one's teeth into
19. Is sick
20. 60's sitcom/90's movie
23. Aardvark's tidbit
24. Lumberjack's tool
25. Possesses
28. Shirt or dress
32. Monet supply?
35. What to make a dep. into
37. Dweeb
38. Allude (to)
40. 60's sitcom/90's movie
43. Individually owned apartment
44. Opposite of a thinker
45. Airport conveyance
46. Sweltering
47. Invisible troublemaker
50. Where the iris is
51. Knot
52. "Hold on a ___!"
54. 60's sitcom/90's movie
63. Artist's work
64. Flip out
65. Jazz lingo
66. Location
67. ___ Dame
68. Preowned
69. Kilt wearer
70. Kills, as a dragon
71. Emperor with a burning ambition?

DOWN

1. Credit card color
2. Clarinet cousin
3. Stitched
4. Laughing ___
5. Where to get a taxi
6. Exclude
7. Butterfly's cousin
8. Liberate
9. Flunky
10. One of the Allman Brothers
11. Operatic solo
12. Baby powder ingredient
13. Otherwise
21. Gerund's end
22. Bonus
25. "Down the ___!" (drinker's toast)
26. Sound before "Gesundheit!"
27. Bloodhound's trail
29. English author Charles
30. 1983 Michael Keaton comedy
31. Ford flop
32. Flaming
33. Pass-the-baton race
34. Product sample's invitation
36. Little bit
39. CPR practitioner
41. Calf, to a cowboy
42. Flying toys
48. Acts as king
49. Born as
51. Den appliance
53. New Orleans cooking style
54. Any Buffalo Bills Super Bowl result
55. Grand, as an adventure
56. Car
57. Hammer or sickle, e.g.
58. "Toodle-oo"
59. Grand Ole ___
60. Workbench clamp
61. At any time
62. Start over

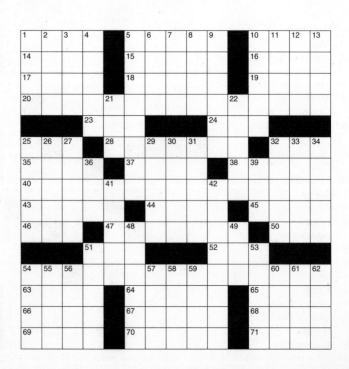

GET MOVING

by Stephanie Spadaccini

ACROSS

1. Freight
6. Watering holes
10. "Puttin' on the ___" (Berlin classic)
14. Completely foreign
15. Early part of the day
16. "Toreador Song," e.g., in "Carmen"
17. River to the Rhône
18. Italian man
19. Rope material
20. Parlors
23. Metal refuse
24. Hwy.
25. Stovetop item
28. Mailing ctrs.
31. "Damn Yankees" temptress
33. Predicament
35. Official proceedings
37. Cartoonist Gross
39. ___ diem (seize the day)
40. Applause, plus
43. Chili con ___
44. Vasco da ___
45. Back talk
46. Where some shoes are made
48. Bring home the bacon
50. "Yo!"
51. Martial arts expert Bruce
52. ___ Cruces, N.M.
54. Spanish rivers
56. Cane
61. Graduation month
64. Poi ingredient
65. Artist Matisse
66. Marco Polo crossed it
67. Catchall abbr.
68. Like certain seals
69. An American, to a Brit
70. Ownership document
71. Gobs

DOWN

1. Elliot, of the Mamas and the Papas
2. Jai ___
3. Uproar
4. Men's room sign
5. "Mourning Becomes Electra" playwright
6. Customs officer's concern
7. Opposite of rich
8. Knight's protection
9. High-hats
10. Cheerleaders' cheers
11. Anger
12. Director Burton or Robbins
13. Knock out, as with a remote
21. Supermodel Campbell
22. Muslim's destination
25. Outcast
26. Go up against
27. Wee
28. French mathematician Blaise
29. 87 or 93 at the pump
30. Go on a hunger strike
32. Pond covering
34. "Fudge!"
36. Years, in old Rome
38. Roseanne's ex
41. Singer Reese
42. Brazilian airline
47. Stored, with "away"
49. Snacks
53. Use Rollerblades
55. Pilfer
56. Lacking strength
57. "Dies ___" (hymn)
58. Concerning
59. Ship's staff
60. Joshes
61. First Chief Justice John
62. Red, white and blue team
63. Writer Anaïs

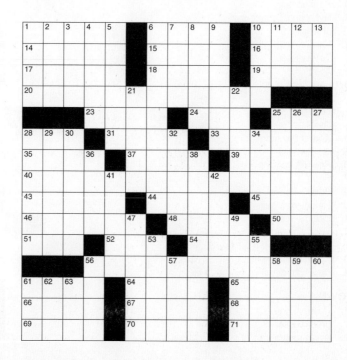

FILTHY HUMOR

by Grace Fabbroni

ACROSS

1. Milky-white gem
5. Turned white
10. Inclusion with a MS.
14. Trucking rig
15. French love
16. Drug ___ (Washington pooh-bah)
17. Patronizing person
18. Sparkling headwear
19. Ladder step
20. Start of a quip
23. Son of Aphrodite
24. Fencing blade
25. Harmony
28. On the up-and-up
31. Rioter's take
32. Joins
34. Hen's pride
37. Middle of the quip
40. Adriatic, e.g.
41. Ryan and Tatum of filmdom
42. Verdi's slave girl
43. Tête-à-têtes
44. Awry
45. Feedback of a sort
47. Like auto shop floors
49. End of the quip
55. ___ and tell
56. Scarlett, for one
57. Snug
59. Sped
60. Heavy volumes
61. Lamb's sobriquet
62. Took advantage of
63. Kasparov's game
64. Red light directive

DOWN

1. C.I.A. predecessor
2. Await judgment
3. To me, in Paris
4. It kept Bizet busy
5. Outdoor lounging area
6. Faulty
7. Temporary use
8. Currency replacing the mark, franc, lira, etc.
9. "Phooey!"
10. Actor's "homework"
11. Sky-blue
12. "À votre ___!"
13. Work unit
21. Word repeated before "again," in a saying
22. Jefferson, religiously
25. Priests' garments
26. Grimace
27. Smidgen
28. Beans in a stew
29. List-ending abbr.
30. Catches on
32. Forearm bone
33. Boris's refusal
34. Actor Estrada
35. 1947 Literature Nobelist André
36. Eat beaver-style
38. Not at all
39. Classic 30's–40's radio comedy
43. Reprimanded, with "out"
44. 100%
45. Group character
46. Taking out the garbage, e.g.
47. Fairy tale villains
48. Bridge declaration
50. University mil. group
51. "Oops!"
52. Reputation
53. Revolver inventor
54. Pinza of the Met
55. Trio after R
58. Prattle

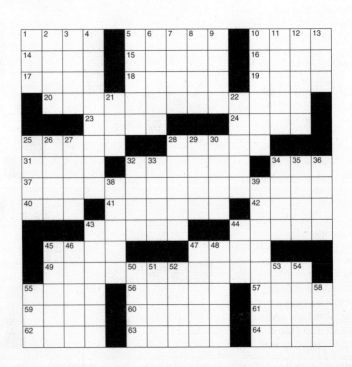

THREE'S COMPANY

by Holden Baker

ACROSS
1. Walk, trot or canter
5. Cheese served with crackers
9. Cavort
13. Speak without notes
15. Loaf about
16. Race track
17. Girl in a children's story
19. Dried up
20. Go on and off, as a traffic light
21. Spain and Portugal
23. Polluted
26. Having round protuberances
27. Hammed it up
28. Irish accent
29. Foremost's partner
30. Try, as a case
31. Go out with
34. Liturgical vestment
35. Mocked
38. Clear (of)
39. Shirts for golfers?
41. Opposite of include
42. Mellowing, as cheese
44. Long-legged shorebird
46. 90's music or fashion
47. These can be winning or losing
49. Scarlet bird
50. Readies, as a pool cue
51. Harold who wrote "Stormy Weather"
52. Harangue
53. Worse than awful
58. Fairy tale's opening word

59. They crisscross Paris
60. Grafting shoot
61. Bambi and kin
62. They may be loose or split
63. Burden

DOWN
1. Joke
2. Commotion
3. State west of Ind.
4. Choice morsels
5. Flaxen-haired
6. Boulder
7. Variety
8. Hamlet's home
9. Citizen Kane's last word
10. Domineering
11. Nobelist Curie
12. Beg
14. Military lodgings

18. Stretched the truth, so to speak
22. Peat locale
23. Trim, as a roast
24. Author Zola
25. Restraint
26. Velveeta maker
28. Comport with
30. Development developments
32. Touch of color
33. Landscaping tool
36. Overconfident
37. Sock menders
40. More slender and graceful
43. Wild llama
45. Acorn tree
46. Joyous celebration
47. Seafood order
48. Macbeth, for one
49. Lady's keepsake to a soldier, once

51. Not up yet
54. Convent dweller
55. Storage container
56. Costello or Grant
57. Printer's widths

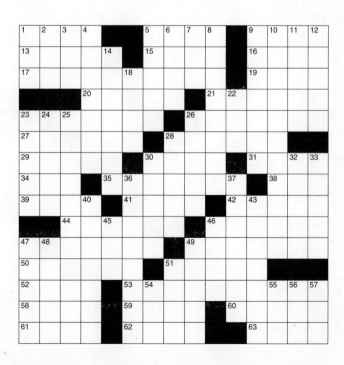

STATE YOUR POSITION

by Alex K. Justin

ACROSS

1. Catches in the act
5. Composer Franz
10. R.N.'s "touch"
13. Singer Guthrie
14. Kind of daisy
15. Where the Mets play
16. 1934 Shirley Temple musical
19. Volcano spew
20. Protest that gets out of hand
21. Bizarre
22. Striped fish
23. Uses to achieve later success
25. Infuriate
28. Place to get all steamed up
29. Hideaway
30. Mode
31. President Lincoln
34. Take time out
38. Hearty mugful
39. Batter's position
40. Battering wind
41. Mailman's beat
42. Plant reproductive bodies
44. One just let out of jail
47. Couples
48. Perfect
49. Bushels
50. "So that's what you meant!"
53. Goldbrick
57. Not so much
58. Kareem ___-Jabbar
59. Back of the neck
60. Take to court
61. Social position
62. Mandated safety sign

DOWN

1. Mars Pathfinder launcher
2. Partner of crafts
3. Ho-hum
4. Prodigal ___
5. 1991 buddy film "Thelma & ___"
6. Montréal team
7. Miami team
8. Writer Rand
9. Deeply blushing
10. Eta follower
11. Skeptical
12. Gives a hoot
15. Six-time Super Bowl coach Don
17. Downer
18. Safe place in the ring
22. Fishhook's end
23. "Band of Gold" singer Freda
24. "___ Lang Syne"
25. "Born Free" lioness
26. It gets hit on the head
27. ___ of passage
28. Condition
30. Rink need
31. Outlawed spray
32. Cotton bundle
33. "First Wives Club" members
35. Moon-landing program
36. Tip-off
37. Subjects of psychoanalysis
41. Highways and byways
42. Nonobvious
43. Deluxe
44. Multivitamins, e.g.
45. Goodbye
46. Shortstop Pee Wee
47. Glazed food item
49. Olympus dwellers
50. Rival of Bon Ami
51. Southwest Indian
52. Help in a heist
54. Servicewoman, briefly
55. Hawks' and Bucks' org.
56. Opposite WSW

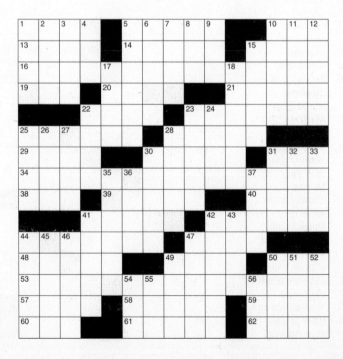

SOUNDS HARD

by Mark Danna

ACROSS

1. Fill in at the office
5. Manias
9. Dressed
13. L.A.-based petroleum giant
14. "Dies ___" (hymn)
15. Salty
16. Corner square in Monopoly
17. Lounge
18. Suddenly leap (at)
19. Second of two pieces of fire truck equipment
22. Take for granted
25. Paragons
26. More drenched minister, at times
30. One who's out of this world?
31. Pays attention to
32. Pie holder
35. Ranges of knowledge
36. Smutty
37. Ending with Cine- or cyclo-
38. Superlative suffix
39. Count ___ & His Orchestra
40. Motive questioner
41. Resentful auctiongoer
43. ___-Lorraine (French region)
46. "Relax, soldiers!"
47. Murmur "a good bad-weather race horse"
51. Thrown for ___
52. Footnote abbr.
53. Morsel for Miss Muffet
57. Former Sen. Sam and family
58. Highway hauler
59. Manipulator
60. Enzyme suffixes
61. Mahogany or maple
62. Prepare, as the way

DOWN

1. ___ Mahal
2. Period in history
3. AT&T alternative
4. Harms the environment
5. Aquarium purifier
6. "I smell ___!"
7. Stun
8. Clairvoyant
9. Less refined
10. Actress Hamilton or Hunt
11. Heavenly host?
12. Salon professionals
15. In-line skates, for short
20. Prayer closer
21. Nixon staffer G. Gordon ___
22. Conscious
23. Tennis star with a palindromic name
24. Limited work assignment
27. Bridge precursor
28. Strange
29. Discourage from acting
32. Bear that's not really a bear
33. Gallic girlfriends
34. Mother-of-pearl
36. Library gizmo
37. International golf competition
39. Bodybuilder's bulges
40. Commend officially
41. Majorettes twirl them
42. Villain, slangily
43. Major oven maker
44. Doozies
45. Rock
48. Morning haze
49. Over, in Österreich
50. Bygone phone call cost
54. Olympics chant
55. Gun, as an engine
56. Rap's Dr. ___

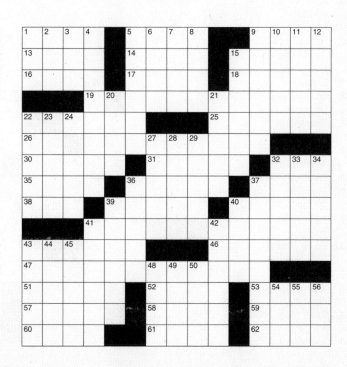

BLISSED OUT

by Mary E. Brindamour

ACROSS

1. "I give up!"
6. Does and bucks
10. Writer Hunter
14. Environment-friendly energy choice
15. Gather leaves
16. It's full of shafts
17. French love affair
18. Products of a 16-Across
19. Customer
20. Hatfield-McCoy affair
21. Place of bliss
23. Stick-on
25. "Here's to you!" and others
26. Hotelier Hilton
28. Make drunk
30. Prefix with cycle
31. Cut into cubes
33. Electrical pioneer Nikola
37. Billions of years
39. House of the Seven Gables site
41. Exhibition
42. Gloomy, in poetry
44. "All sales are ___"
46. Playwright Burrows
47. Flood embankment
49. Displayed ennui
51. Entertain, as with stories
54. 1924 Ferber novel
55. Place of bliss
58. Irish offshoot
61. ___-mutuel
62. Worker protection org.
63. From Mars, say
64. Margin
65. Airline to Tel Aviv
66. Sat and did nothing
67. Requisite
68. Specks
69. Pre-1917 Russian rulers

DOWN

1. It has its academy in Colo. Spr.
2. Alaskan outpost
3. Place of bliss
4. Cosmetician Estee
5. Flub
6. Openly salivate
7. Make, as money
8. Managed, with "out"
9. Adjusts, as a clock
10. Copies
11. Travel papers
12. Regarding
13. Hardly hipsters
21. African waterbeds
22. Plant anchorer
24. No-goodnik
26. Prompted
27. ___ about (circa)
28. Contradict
29. Paradise
32. Eatery
34. Place of bliss
35. Earring site
36. In wonderment
38. On the payroll
40. Giuliani, e.g.
43. Depend (on)
45. Inventor's workplace
48. Said no to
50. Exercises, as authority
51. Come of age
52. Get around
53. Stuff to the gills
54. Flippered animals
56. Nobel Peace Prize city
57. One of the five W's
59. Séance holder
60. Quashes
63. River islet

QUIT STALLING

by Stephanie Spadaccini

ACROSS

1. "___ the Horrible"
6. Challenge to a gunslinger
10. Out-of-focus picture
14. Wonderland girl
15. Relaxation
16. Country road
17. Evasive answer #1
20. Have a feeling
21. Prefix with linear
22. Swiss peak
25. Twain's "The Gilded ___"
26. Wailing woman, in folklore
28. Tell
30. Insertion symbol
31. Race track shape
32. Haying machine
33. Droop
36. Evasive answer #2
40. ___ gratia artis
41. Nonsecular types
42. Jason's ship
43. Members of a chess line
44. Rough, as terrain
46. "Thank you for ___ . . ."
49. Author Rand
50. Golfer Ernie
51. Founder of the Soviet Union
52. Plot of land
54. Evasive answer #3
60. Capri, e.g.
61. Detroit products
62. Florida city
63. ___-do-well

64. Overpublicize
65. "I understand!"

DOWN

1. "Bali ___"
2. Entirely
3. TV actor Gerard
4. Does film work
5. Warm up, as food
6. Thick
7. Garden tool
8. White ___ ghost
9. Internet
10. Deepest azure
11. Gate holder
12. Knot
13. Knot again
18. "Picnic" planner
19. Obstinate
22. Scent
23. TV actor Burton
24. "Hamlet" and "Macbeth"

26. Mild, as weather
27. Neighborhood
29. Priestly garb
30. Playbill listings
32. Existence
33. Suit material
34. Broadway backer
35. Merchandise
37. "Seinfeld" lady
38. Open wide
39. Base in baseball
43. First-grade book
44. Pitcher Nolan
45. Clear, as a drain
46. Killed
47. German Hermann
48. Leg joint
49. Get up
52. Canvas cover
53. Mexican sandwich

55. Oh, in Heidelberg
56. ___ Men's Health Crisis
57. Tit for ___
58. Yalie
59. Stinker

WORKING VACATION

by Arthur S. Verdesca

ACROSS

1. Capital of Azerbaijan
5. ___ Kett of early comics
9. Confronts
14. X___xylophone
15. Statutes
16. Nonsensical
17. Leave in, editorially
18. Explorer called "the Red"
19. Kind of orange
20. With 34-, 43- and 58-Across, message on a tourist's postcard
23. Chou En-___
24. Bout outcome, briefly
25. River at Ghent
26. Strike caller
29. After
32. Truck track
34. See 20-Across
39. Composer Stravinsky
40. Moray, e.g.
41. Lendl of tennis
43. See 20-Across
48. Ordinal suffix
49. Card game start
50. Born: Fr.
51. Airline with the old slogan "Up, up and away"
54. Broadcast
56. Oversized
58. See 20-Across
65. Put ___ to (end)
66. Surrealist Salvador
67. Gym socks may have one
68. India's first P.M.
69. "Holy moly!"
70. What's holding things up
71. Like Gatsby
72. Actress Russo
73. Root in Hawaiian cookery

DOWN

1. Wingding
2. Nick and Nora's dog
3. Chicken ___ (deep-fried dish)
4. "Don't open ___ Christmas!"
5. Mournful
6. Scarlett's home
7. Baby branch
8. Broad necktie
9. Discover
10. Med. course
11. Carp
12. Hostile force
13. Tennis champ Monica
21. Back of the neck
22. Gumbo
26. A.P. rival
27. Prefix with bucks or phone
28. Ship's front
30. Part of a rose
31. Preppy's fabric
33. Significantly underweight
35. At liberty
36. "What ___ can I say?"
37. Uniform
38. Lightly cooked
42. Actress Carrie
44. "Don't move!"
45. Toledo's home
46. Trip to the airport, say
47. Nobelist Wiesel
51. Nasal tone
52. More prudent
53. "___ World Turns"
55. Less polite
57. Basic Halloween costume
59. Jewish wedding dance
60. Carry on
61. Vivacity
62. ___ St. Vincent Millay
63. Din
64. Hence

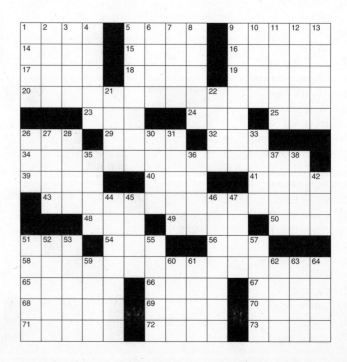

STAY A WHILE

by Gregory E. Paul

ACROSS

1. With gold trim
5. Jewish text
10. Breakfast restaurant chain
14. Dr. Frankenstein's assistant
15. Scent
16. Taboo
17. "Psycho" setting
19. Buttonhole
20. Elvis's Graceland, e.g.
21. In dire __
23. Sudden swelling
26. Contents of a playground box
27. Radio tube gas
30. Aardvark's nibble
32. Razz
35. Used
36. Winslow Homer, e.g.
38. Day in Jerusalem
39. Nabokov heroine
40. Hooey
41. Bachelor's last words
42. Stimpy's pal
43. Emissary
44. Winged pest
45. Jump out of the way
47. Opposite WSW
48. Pick up on
49. Replaceable shoe part
51. Snares
53. Dagwood's lady
56. Rag
60. Item often kept on hand?
61. Title setting for a Neil Simon play
64. Hurler Hershiser
65. Egg on
66. Tear up
67. Yarborough of the Daytona 500

68. "Lorna __" (1869 novel)
69. Slices of history

DOWN

1. Taunt
2. Certain supermarkets, for short
3. Sen. Trent __
4. Benedict Arnold's crime
5. Bronco buster
6. Aztec treasure
7. Go bad
8. Iowa State University site
9. Puts a stop to
10. Loony
11. "White Christmas" setting, 1942
12. "Put a lid __!"
13. Partner of pans

18. Flabbergast
22. Threadbare
24. Auto repair shop
25. Contest contestant
27. Obie, for one
28. Calgary Stampede, e.g.
29. Title setting for a 1932 Oscar film
31. Hairdresser, at times
33. Fountain treats
34. Ham it up
36. London libation
37. Envision
40. Run in the wash
44. Signal with the hands
46. Not rough
48. Hot tubs
50. Biochemical compound

52. Swifts "__ of a Tub"
53. Univ. hotshot
54. Money in Milan
55. "Sesame Street" Muppet
57. Bleacher feature
58. Sicilian rumbler
59. Zinfandels
62. Sgt.'s mail drop
63. Buddhist sect

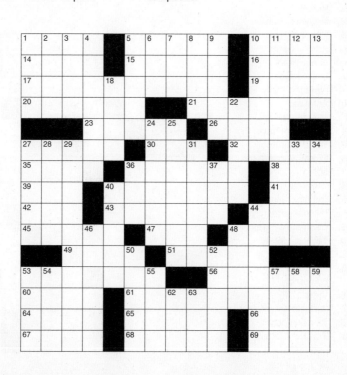

LEGAL-ESE

by Mark Moldowsky

ACROSS

1. Birthplace of Columbus
6. Doesn't exist
10. Dog-paddle, say
14. Baking chambers
15. Headline
16. "___ you don't!"
17. What the jury does after deliberating
20. Poker starter
21. Small and weak
22. Swearing to tell the truth, and others
23. The highest degree
24. Perjured oneself
25. Facility
26. Sleuth, informally
27. Not real
29. Michael Douglas, to Kirk
32. Heavenly hunter
35. Passes easily
36. Knight's wife, in olden times
37. Legal reach, metaphorically
40. Actress Lanchester
41. "___ Misbehavin' "
42. Siskel's partner
43. Wreak vengeance on
44. Chicken style
45. Big blast maker
46. Biblical garden
48. Cash substitutes
50. Test-___ treaty
53. A Beatle
55. It's clicked on a computer
56. Vigor
57. Judge's cry
60. Thirteen popes
61. Toward shelter, nautically

62. Word with ear or peace
63. Dict. items
64. Antidrinking org.
65. + end

DOWN

1. Tennis star Ivanisevic
2. News basis
3. Under, in poetry
4. A single time
5. Baseball bat wood
6. Philately offering
7. Awaits sentencing
8. Dark blue
9. Number of coins in an Italian fountain
10. Ice cream drinks
11. January store happening

12. Distance between belt notches, maybe
13. Witty sayings
18. Like the "Iliad" and "Odyssey"
19. Wander
24. Songstress Horne
25. Sunrise direction
26. Ceremonial gown
28. Bulk
30. "Rubáiyát" poet
31. Salamander
32. Designer Cassini
33. Part to play
34. Rather than
35. Gallic girlfriend
36. Money owed
38. Reason for postponement
39. Egg producers
44. Critic Walter
45. Composer's output

47. Chemise
49. Marveled aloud
50. Shoe designer Magli
51. Broadcast
52. ___ Dame
53. Auctioned off
54. Shade giver
55. "To Live and Die ___" ('85 film)
56. West German capital
58. "___ shocked!"
59. Spy org.

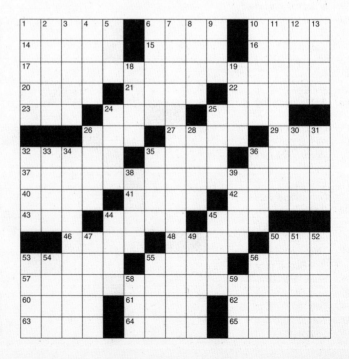

DON'T MOVE

by Gerald R. Ferguson

ACROSS

1. Quark's place
5. Some are filled out
10. Org. for 7-Down
14. Command on a submarine
15. Beethoven dedicatee
16. Get ___ the ground floor
17. "Stop" sign
20. Costa del ___
21. Cleanse
22. One of the Brothers Karamazov
23. "Unforgettable" singer
24. Gas or elec., e.g.
25. To pieces
28. Lustrous fabric
30. Sailor
33. Assail
34. Ted's role on "Cheers"
35. "Dies ___"
36. "Stop" sign
40. Connecticut Ivy Leaguers
41. ___ de la Cite
42. Marconi's invention
43. Cub's home
44. To whom Tinker threw
46. Alamogordo event
47. Bouillabaisse, e.g.
48. Table d'___
50. Chairs on poles
53. Angler's luck
54. Guy's date
57. "Stop" sign
60. German article
61. Colorful rock
62. "Pistol Packin' ___"
63. Cherished
64. Wankel engine part
65. Procedure part

DOWN

1. Tacks on
2. Novice: Var.
3. Track shape
4. Kitten's cry
5. Untamed
6. Mount of ___ (site near Jerusalem)
7. Astronaut Sally
8. N.Y.C. sports venue
9. When to sow
10. This meant nothing to Nero
11. Operating without ___ (taking risks)
12. Skyrocket
13. "The King ___"
18. Three sheets to the wind
19. Ugandan dictator
23. Game featuring shooters
24. Where Provo is
25. Invited
26. English dramatist George
27. Supped at home
29. Starwort
30. School division
31. Watering hole
32. Infatuate
35. Furious
37. Exceptional, as a restaurant or hotel
38. Went by plane
39. Gadget for cheese
44. Sicilian volcano
45. Religion of Japan
47. Not a spendthrift
49. Aquatic mammal
50. Scurried
51. Buffalo's lake
52. Actress Merrill
53. Tuckered out
54. Midge
55. Crowning point
56. "Able to ___ tall buildings . . ."
58. Freudian factor
59. Early hrs.

HOMONYM TRIO

by Jeff Herrington

ACROSS

1. Sluggers' stats
5. Theme of this puzzle
10. Capital of Italia
14. Burn soother
15. Filibuster, in a way
16. Hawaiian music makers
17. Editor's definition of this puzzle's theme
20. Prevent legally
21. Popular beverage brand
22. Shea nine
25. More crafty
26. Allowable
30. Beckon
33. University of Maine site
34. ___-do-well
35. Dickens protagonist
38. Mapmaker's definition of this puzzle's theme
42. Compass heading
43. Pseudonymous short-story writer
44. Backing for an exhibit
45. Peaceful
47. Sentient
48. Insurance giant
51. Negative in Nuremberg
53. Competed in the Hambletonian
56. Ribeye, e.g.
60. Physician's definition of this puzzle's theme
64. Bank claim
65. Battery part
66. Former second in command
67. Driver's license prerequisite
68. The ___ Prayer
69. Interested look

DOWN

1. Genre for the Notorious B.I.G.
2. Depressed
3. Charged particles
4. Split-off group
5. Stylish auto
6. Man-mouse link
7. Back muscle, familiarly
8. Redding of 60's soul
9. "Open 24 hours" sign, maybe
10. Muss up
11. Animal with zebra-striped legs
12. Actress Oberon
13. Questioner
18. Indian drum
19. Political cartoonist Thomas
23. Kid's make-believe telephone
24. Elude the doorman
26. Canter
27. Ayatollah's land
28. Dunce cap, essentially
29. ___ pinch
31. Where St. Mark's Cathedral is
32. Investment vehicle, for short
35. Famous tower locale
36. Roman road
37. See 49-Down
39. Enzyme suffix
40. Shanty
41. Bird's cry
45. Purpose
46. "Phooey!"
48. Not perfectly upright
49. With 37-Down, famous W.W. II correspondent
50. Big handbags
52. Wight and Man
54. List shortener
55. Singer Martin, to friends
57. Therefore
58. In awe
59. Basketball's Malone
61. Neither's companion
62. Do basic arithmetic
63. Society column word

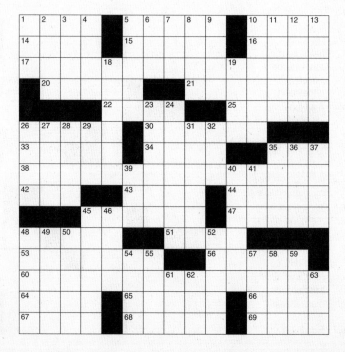

POOL PARTY

by Brendan Emmett Quigley

ACROSS
1. Procter & Gamble bar
6. Native Alaskan
11. Spoil
14. Midwest airport hub
15. Sergeant at TV's Fort Baxter
16. Diamonds
17. Place to place a wallet or handkerchief
19. ___ Na Na
20. Thanksgiving meat request
21. "Entry of Christ Into Brussels" painter James
23. Scott Adams's put-upon comics hero
27. Nautical spar
29. Body parts shaped like punching bags
30. W.W. II Philippine battle site
31. Horse in a harness race
32. 1924 Ferber novel
33. Little newt
36. It's NNW of Oklahoma City
37. Rounded lumps
38. Nicholas I or II, e.g.
39. Mule of song
40. Nash's two-L beast
41. Hardly elegant
42. Easy two-pointers
44. Concert halls
45. Starts of tourneys
47. Last course
48. Peres's predecessor
49. "___ That a Shame"
50. Eggs

51. "Come on!"
58. ___ canto (singing style)
59. Characteristic
60. Confuse
61. Right-angle joint
62. Steinbeck migrants
63. Dapper

DOWN
1. ___ a plea
2. "Now I see!"
3. Beatnik's exclamation
4. Skill
5. Sweetheart's assent
6. Cancel, as a launch
7. Drub
8. Lodge member
9. Luau instrument
10. Alternative to a purse

11. Err on stage
12. Cause for blessing?
13. Get ready for battle again
18. Average figures
22. Org. for Bulls and Bullets
23. Fools
24. Ex-Mrs. Trump
25. Four-time Emmy-winning comedienne
26. Ran, as colors
27. ___ the Hutt, of "Star Wars"
28. Medical suffix
30. Certain mikes
32. Knee hits
34. Mountebank
35. Lovers' engagement
37. Rather morose
38. Suns

40. Deceiving
41. Nuclear treaty subject
43. "The Greatest!"
44. ___ cava (path to the heart)
45. Explore
46. "Bolero" composer
47. They're losing propositions
49. French friend
52. Bother
53. ___ tai (drink)
54. Nutritional abbr.
55. N.Y.C. summer clock setting
56. Model Carol
57. Lock opener

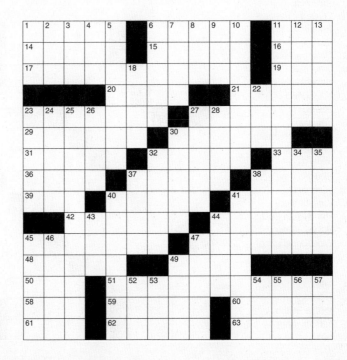

WORD FOR WORD

by Gregory E. Paul

ACROSS

1. Farm structure
5. Kon-Tiki wood
10. Boutique
14. Rev. Roberts
15. From the East
16. Windex target
17. Conjointly
19. Killer whale film
20. Till bill
21. Plant part
22. Ham
24. Certain pints
25. Vessel
26. Novelist-screenwriter Eric
29. Person in need of salvation
32. Places to buy cold cuts
33. Dugout
34. Showtime rival
35. Greatly
36. Where Joan of Arc died
37. Wilde's "The Ballad of Reading ___"
38. Catty remark?
39. Vine fruit
40. Snorkeler's sight
41. "O Pioneers!" setting
43. Talkative
44. Joins the team?
45. Stable newborn
46. Insignia
48. Sheryl Crow's "___ Wanna Do"
49. Kind of story
52. Handyman Bob
53. Bobby Vinton hit
56. Word after pig or before horse
57. Burdened
58. Tittle
59. Ribald
60. Works in the cutting room
61. Midterm, e.g.

DOWN

1. Part of London or Manhattan
2. Teheran's land
3. Rural route
4. Like a centenarian
5. Back-and-forth
6. Grate expectations?
7. Actor Neeson
8. ___ Diego
9. "Father Knows Best" family name
10. Lampoons
11. Sidney Sheldon TV series
12. Some time ago
13. Fruit cocktail fruit
18. Tropical getaways
23. Pal, Down Under
24. Dismounted
25. "We'll go to ___, and eat bologna . . ."
26. Rhett's last words
27. Free-for-all
28. Detailed account
29. Singer Nyro or Branigan
30. German sub
31. Candy on a stick, informally
33. Parts of wine bottles
36. Look like
37. Soccer score
39. Enter a Pillsbury contest
40. Mountain range
42. Hero of early French ballads
43. Punctuation marks
45. Armada
46. Like Satan
47. Bog
48. German auto
49. Gin flavor
50. Scoreboard stat
51. Cop's milieu.
54. Youth
55. Bridle part

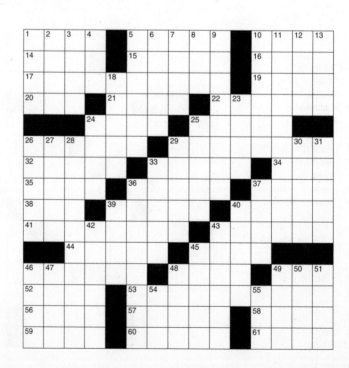

STRIP TEASE

by Elizabeth C. Gorski

ACROSS

1. Utters
5. Military plane acronym
10. Desertlike
14. Wyoming neighbor
15. Striped critter
16. Hurting
17. State of financial independence
19. CAT ___
20. Singer Lopez
21. Kett of old comics
22. Little guitars
23. Singer Cara
25. Guard
27. It's a stitch!
29. Mint and sage
32. Stadium sounds
35. Basketball hoop site, often
39. Acorn, in 2020?
40. "Surfin' ___" (Beach Boys hit)
41. Gandhi's title
42. Ryan's "Love Story" co-star
43. Russian space station
44. Puzzle
45. 4:1, e.g.
46. Mubarak's predecessor
48. Recipe direction
50. Some Broadway shows
54. Overhead shot
57. Last name in spydom
59. "There ought to be ___!"
61. Suggest itself (to)
63. Thrift shop stipulation
64. "The Birdcage" co-star
66. Possess
67. Whitney Houston's "All the Man That ___"
68. Verve
69. Parrots
70. Chooses actors
71. E-mail command

DOWN

1. Winter bird food
2. Video arcade name
3. Arafat of the P.L.O.
4. Wallflower's characteristic
5. Much-publicized drug
6. Existed
7. Helps in dirty deeds
8. El Greco's birthplace
9. Underworld figure
10. Guarantee
11. Ice cream parlor order
12. "Dies ___"
13. TV rooms
18. ___ qua non
24. 1991 Tony winner Daisy
26. "Take ___ Train"
28. When repeated, a fish
30. Like a worn tire
31. T-bar sights
32. Jamaican exports
33. Pacific Rim region
34. Computer part
36. Joplin piece
37. 24-hr. conveniences
38. Certain exams, for short
41. Prefix with physical
45. The Scriptures
47. Gets up
49. "___ Fire" (Springsteen hit)
51. Wired, so to speak
52. "The George & ___ Show" (former talk show)
53. Fills up
55. Union rate
56. Chinese province
57. Joker's gibe
58. Rush job notation
60. Stimulate
62. Rip apart
65. Want ___

"OK, NE QUESTIONS?"

by Stephanie Spadaccini

ACROSS

1. 27, to 3
5. Virgule
10. St. Nick accessory
14. The top
15. "Remember the ___!"
16. "Ars Amatoria" poet
17. Surgical site in the Beaver State?
19. Kid's phrase of request
20. Chang's Siamese twin
21. Itch
22. Full moon color
24. Commedia dell'___
25. Rapper who co-starred in "New Jack City"
26. Le Carre character George
29. Methodology
32. Estate papers
33. Gunk
34. Champagne Tony of golf
36. ___ vera
37. Middays
38. Money to tide one over
39. It's west of N.C.
40. Just
41. "What ___ I do?"
42. Nielsen stats
44. Comic Charles Nelson ___
45. Unpleasant task
46. Hospital unit
47. Declarer
50. Swiss river
51. "___ is me!"
54. Glitzy sign
55. Doc from the Old Line State?
58. Cartoonist Al
59. Chorus girls?
60. The first: Abbr.
61. Fashion's Klensch
62. 1956 Four Lads hit "___ Much!"
63. It's just for openers

DOWN

1. Supergarb
2. "___ the housetop . . ." (Christmas lyric)
3. Arctic Ocean sighting
4. Phone line abbr.
5. ___-pants (wise guy)
6. Jessica of "Frances"
7. Right-hand person
8. ___-cone
9. Decorated officers
10. Driver's license in the Gem State?
11. Russian "John"
12. Engine knock
13. Actress McClurg
18. Fishing gear
23. ___ room
24. Sound system in the Keystone State?
25. Humor not for dummies
26. Quite a hit
27. Distance runner
28. Actress Massey
29. Chlorinated waters
30. 1988 Olympics site
31. Inconsequential
33. Pagoda sounds
35. "Handy" man
37. Rural
41. Goddess of agriculture
43. Suffix with elephant
44. Least cooked
46. "Yippee!"
47. Suffix with utter
48. ___ piccata
49. Kin of "Uh-oh!"
50. Envelope abbr.
51. Alert
52. Leave off
53. Periphery
56. "Strange Magic" rock band
57. 1988 Dennis Quaid remake

DON'T RULE ANYTHING OUT

by Jonathan Schmalzbach

ACROSS

1. Support
5. Hindu gentleman
9. Indonesian island
14. Nautical direction
15. Part of the eye
16. Mirror ___
17. Charlemagne's legacy
20. Lepidopterist's equipment
21. Corrida cries
22. Condemned
23. Marking float
24. Tiny memory measures
25. "Nothing ___!"
27. James Buchanan, notably
31. Reign noted for magnificent porcelain
33. Actress Hagen
34. Commentators' page
35. Cricket sides
36. Play start
37. German direction
38. Virginia's nickname
42. Farewells
44. Chips in?
45. Rara ___
46. Semicircles
47. Gene Kelly's activity in the 30-Down
50. Hammett pooch
51. Stage of history
54. Disney realm
57. Draw a bead on
58. Subsequently
59. Venom
60. Cache
61. Stitches
62. Charon's river

DOWN

1. Where to take a Volkswagen for a spin
2. Shampoo ingredient
3. Breton, for one
4. Crucial
5. What John Scopes taught
6. Former Majority leader Dick
7. Partiality
8. Milit. branch
9. Coarse fodder grass
10. Levy
11. Impair
12. Bogeyman
13. Army surgeon Walter
18. Spherical
19. Pronouncement
23. Nickname for the Cowboys' hometown

24. One who sings the part of Boris Godunov
25. Boozehound
26. "And ___ grow on"
27. They were big in the 40's
28. "A Tale of Two Cities" heroine
29. Director Preminger et al.
30. See 47-Across
31. ___ synthesizer
32. Stem joints
36. Termites' kin
38. Render unnecessary
39. Fibbing
40. Forked-tail swallows
41. From early Peru

43. Buxom blonde of 50's TV
46. Crooked
47. B.&O. stops
48. "___ a New High" (1937 Lily Pons song)
49. Verne's captain
50. Lumbago, e.g.
51. Blue-pencil
52. ___-poly
53. Big Board's brother: Abbr.
55. "___ Not Unusual!"
56. Literary monogram

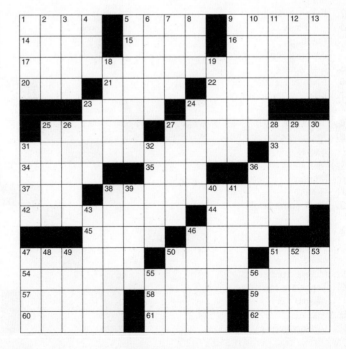

GLASS MENAGERIE?

ACROSS

1. Indian title of respect
6. Love handles, essentially
10. Gad about
14. "Fur ___" (Beethoven dedication)
15. Clarence Thomas's garb
16. Second word of many limericks
17. It's not as threatening as it looks
19. Give up
20. Current strength
21. Antiaircraft fire
23. London lavatory
24. "Rocky ___"
25. ___ A Sketch (drawing toy)
26. Old age, in old times
27. Italian cheese
31. ___ Major (southern constellation)
35. Mat victory
36. River of Russia
37. Man ___ (famous race horse)
38. Jive talkin'
40. Running shoe name
41. Marquand's Mr. ___
42. Rotter
43. Does some lawn work
44. Disappear through camouflage
46. Mineral springs
48. Tended to the weeds
49. "High ___" (Anderson play)
50. Photo ___ (camera sessions)
53. Repudiate
56. Horrid
58. It's put off at the bakery
59. Shooter's target
61. Change for a C-note
62. Roof overhang
63. Homes for hatchlings
64. Philosopher
65. Exceeded the limit
66. Gaggle members

DOWN

1. Flower part
2. Bowie's last stand
3. Swimmer in the Congo
4. "Now it's clear!"
5. Additions to an ice cream sundae
6. North Pole–like
7. Theater section
8. Burrows of the theater
9. Chewing out
10. Geologist
11. ___-Day (vitamin brand)
12. Australian hard-rock band
13. Like a milquetoast
18. Party game pin-on
22. New Deal prog.
25. "___ go bragh"
28. Math subject
29. Money brought in
30. Pub quaffs
31. Toothed item
32. Roll call misser
33. Hoops great Archibald
34. Lou Gehrig nickname, with "the"
35. Seat cover
38. Arts' partner
39. Touch down
43. Bringing in
45. ___ Jones
46. Hung around
47. Splendor
50. Corpulent plus
51. Draws, as a line on a graph
52. Good judgment
53. Pencil-and-paper game
54. Brainstorm
55. Carol
56. Garroway of early TV
57. "The African Queen" scriptwriter
60. Drink like Fido

FOREIGN PHRASEOLOGY

by Robert Zimmerman

ACROSS

1. Bid
6. Mesa dweller
10. Nod off
14. Site of Cnossus
15. Big name in cosmetics
16. German biographer ___ Ludwig
17. "___ looking at you, kid"
18. Lady's man
19. Movers
20. Quirky
21. Impressive achievement
24. Sorbonne, e.g.
26. Tire channel
27. Peer, to his servant
29. Plant with a medicinal root
33. More than peeved
34. Charles's domain
35. Hemispheric assn.
37. Ready to come off the stove
38. Examined, as before a robbery
39. Skip
40. Business mag
41. Lawn
42. "The Taming of the Shrew" setting
43. Spy's byword
45. Police datum
46. Assistance
47. Like toast
48. Final stroke
53. Fate
56. The "A" in A.D.
57. Film ___
58. Pan-fry
60. Harness part
61. Gusto
62. Greek satirist
63. These may be fine
64. On the main
65. Driving hazard

DOWN

1. Cuatro y cuatro
2. N.F.L. receiver Biletnikoff
3. Tropical viper
4. Bastille Day season
5. Give back
6. World Court site, with "The"
7. Finished
8. Thoreau subject
9. Confined, as in wartime
10. Give, as time
11. Gen. Bradley
12. Over-the-counter cold remedy
13. Otherwise
22. Aged
23. Ado
25. ___ d'Azur (French Riviera)
27. Certain skirt
28. Actor Jeremy
29. Long-winded
30. Nouvelle Caledonie and others
31. Pseudonym
32. Julius Caesar's first name
34. W.W. II enlistee
36. Immediately, in the E.R.
38. Sideboard
39. Sculls
41. Part of a crossword
42. Clergymen
44. Poultry offerings
45. Compass tracing
47. Magna ___
48. Dear, as a signorina
49. Unique person
50. Military group
51. "Anything ___" (1934 or 1987 musical)
52. Levitate
54. Siouan tribe
55. Camp shelter
59. Be sick

READ THAT TO ME AGAIN

by Stephanie Spadaccini

ACROSS

1. Stage between egg and pupa
6. "Durn it!"
10. Head of hair, slangily
13. "Silas Marner" author
14. Exploiters
16. Eggs
17. Teensy-weensy piece of beef?
19. Seat in St. Paul's
20. ___ Rosa, Calif.
21. 1984 World Series champs
23. The sun
26. Johnnie Ray hit of the 50's
27. Biblical king
28. Sleazy
30. Sandlot sport
33. Cottonlike fiber
34. Without
35. Actress ___ Dawn Chong
36. Got 100 on
37. Dot on a monitor
38. Tiny bit
39. ___-de-France
40. Radius, ulna, etc.
41. U.C.L.A. player
42. Big North Carolina industry
44. "Dirty Rotten Scoundrels" actress ___ Headly
45. Kind of bean
46. Old French coin
47. ___ es Salaam
48. Tom Canty, in a Mark Twain book
50. Pedestals, e.g.
52. Mornings, for short
53. What stand-up comics do to keep their material shiny?
58. Soupy Sales missile
59. Long bout
60. Vicinities
61. Catalogue contents
62. Some P.T.A. members
63. Long (for)

DOWN

1. Moon craft, for short
2. Actress MacGraw
3. ___ Tin Tin
4. "Comment allez-___?"
5. Embassy worker
6. Name for a cowpoke
7. Movie pooch
8. Society page word
9. Like a proper rescuee
10. Ride an engine-powered bike?
11. Finished
12. Furry feet
15. Poodle and dirndl, e.g.
18. Professor 'iggins
22. Sailor
23. Sea route
24. Delphic shrine
25. "My gold dress isn't back from the cleaners yet" and others?
27. Sharpens
29. Caesar of "Caesar's Hour"
30. At ___ and sevens
31. Chicana
32. Horseshoes shot
34. Sal of "Giant"
37. Instant picture
38. Anger
40. They're big in gyms
41. Colorful, crested bird
43. Strike lightly
44. "No kidding!"
46. MS. enclosures
48. Madonna's "___ Don't Preach"
49. In the center of
50. Dallas's nickname
51. Achy
54. Meadow
55. Mauna ___
56. It may be pulled in charades
57. ID digits

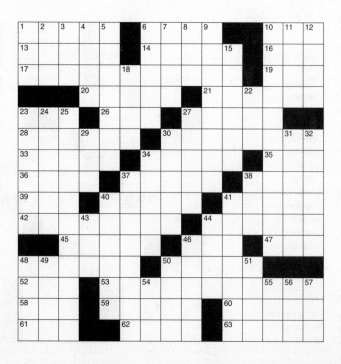

PAY UP

by Fred Piscop

ACROSS

1. The Hatfields or the McCoys
5. Trip to Mecca
9. Quench
14. Any one of three English rivers
15. "Summertime," e.g., in "Porgy and Bess"
16. Jazzman's cue
17. Woolen wear
20. Bizarre
21. Small ball
22. Makes certain
25. Long, long time
26. Toyota model
28. Govt. agent
32. Fortify, as a town
37. Brit's reply in agreement
38. Spot in a supermarket
41. Cowboys' entertainment
42. Said again
43. Not new
44. Scold
46. Court
47. Riddles
53. Names
58. A lot of Shakespeare's writing
59. Ambassador's stand-in
62. You can dig it
63. Island near Kauai
64. Touches lightly, as with a hanky
65. Soccer shoe
66. Ending with cable or candy
67. Command to Fido

DOWN

1. Drink served with marshmallows
2. Hawaiian feasts
3. Aides-de-camp: Abbr.
4. India's first P.M.
5. "Scots Wha ___" (Burns poem)
6. Sheet music abbr.
7. Goes kaput
8. Quartz variety
9. Oft-televised bishop
10. Polygraph flunker
11. Westernmost Aleutian
12. Canal to the Baltic
13. Raison d'___
18. Debussy's "La ___"
19. Rider's "Stop!"
23. "What's this, Pedro?"
24. "Star Trek" helmsman
27. Kind of lab dish
28. Melt ingredient
29. Catcher's catcher
30. Suit to ___
31. Taped eyeglasses wearer
32. Very light brown
33. Conductance units
34. "Venerable" English writer
35. Passed with flying colors
36. Bout outcome, in brief
37. "___ Sera, Sera"
39. Give up
40. Begin bidding
44. Baskin-Robbins purchase
45. Show off on the slopes
46. Isle of ___
48. Sweet-as-apple-cider girl
49. Diagrams
50. French Revolution figure Jean Paul
51. Microscopic creature
52. Giving a little lip
53. Electrical letters
54. Sen. Gramm
55. Noggin
56. Killer whale
57. Coal-rich European region
60. Home-financing org.
61. "Fe fi fo ___!"

BIG ADVICE

by Stephanie Spadaccini

ACROSS

1. "Woe is me!"
5. A wanted man, maybe
9. Miss in the comics
14. ___ Le Pew
15. Oldsmobile, e.g.
16. Sound during hay fever season
17. 47-stringed instrument
18. Flair
19. "Jurassic Park" sound
20. Parental advice, part 1
23. ___ Moines
24. "O Sole ___"
25. Antislavery leader Turner
26. Call to Bo-peep
27. Once more, country-style
29. Name
32. See-through wrap
35. Scandinavian capital
36. "The Official Preppy Handbook" author Birnbach
37. Advice, part 2
40. ___ Major
41. Economist Smith
42. Listens to
43. "See ya!"
44. Utopia
45. Served with a meal
46. Choice of sizes: Abbr.
47. Not their
48. Twaddle
51. End of the advice
57. "Silas Marner" author
58. Derby distance, maybe
59. Small field
60. Training group
61. "Zip-___-Doo-Dah"
62. Wedding wear
63. Injured sneakily
64. Back talk
65. Mesozoic and others

DOWN

1. Garden pest
2. What all partygoers eventually take
3. After, in Avignon
4. Fall mo.
5. Flier Earhart
6. "Where's ___?"
7. "Sure, why not?"
8. Letterman rival
9. Hit game of 1980
10. Showy display
11. Call to a mate
12. Search, as a beach
13. Long (for)
21. Mideasterner
22. Merger
26. Where Bear Bryant coached, informally
27. Oriental
28. Grab (onto)
29. ___-a-minute (call rate)
30. Previously owned
31. Chorale part
32. The short end
33. Wrong
34. Floral gift
35. Ye ___ Tea Shoppe
36. Told a whopper
38. Soup scoop
39. "Ta-da!"
44. Hammed it up
45. 90's group with the hit "Killing Me Softly," with "the"
46. Boutique
47. Looks at boldly
48. Track car
49. Open-air rooms
50. Skins
51. Isthmus
52. Pearl Buck heroine
53. Coastal flooding factor
54. Holiday season, for short
55. Verdi heroine
56. 90's party

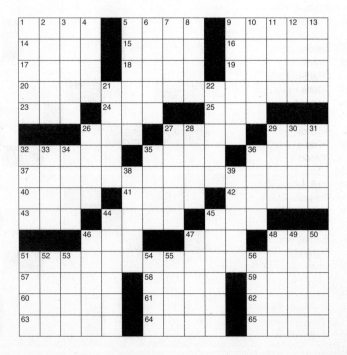

DOUBLE CROSSING

by Frank Longo

ACROSS

1. Top piece of a two-piece
4. Italian seaport
11. Timber wood
14. "Alley ___"
15. Zoom-in shot
16. Chinese principle
17. Sex determinant
19. ___ rampage
20. Ready to go
21. Taste test label
23. 200 milligrams, to a jeweler
25. Funnyman Philips
28. Not have ___ in the world
29. Spinks defeater, 1978
30. Parallel bar exercises
32. Not nude
33. Complicated situations
37. Debussy contemporary
39. Treasure hunter's declaration
43. Pen
44. Parti-colored
46. Quite the expert
49. Having conflicting allegiances
51. ___ du Diable
52. Kind of fool
54. Wood splitter
55. Quite the expert
57. For adults only
59. Tickle one's fancy
61. Play (with)
62. Twenty-somethings
67. Jargon suffix
68. Earth, wind or fire
69. Squid secretion
70. Texas-Oklahoma boundary river
71. Tennis volleys
72. Gypsy Rose ___

DOWN

1. Word with band or sand
2. Dutton's sitcom role
3. "Art is long, life is short," e.g.
4. Astronaut Carpenter
5. Soprano Gluck
6. Blotto
7. Suffix with lion
8. Rock's ___ Speedwagon
9. Feeling the effects of Novocaine
10. "Don Giovanni," for one
11. Like Schoenberg's music
12. Bullock of "Speed"
13. Took in, in a way
18. Genetic stuff
22. Say "yes" to
23. Auto shaft, slangily
24. "Family Ties" boy
26. Anonymous man
27. Moonfish
31. Fruit/tree connector
34. Deemed appropriate
35. Miscalculate
36. "In Living Color" segment
38. Prefix with propyl
40. Greek portico
41. Salad dressing ingredient
42. Boob tube, in Britain: Var.
45. Hankering
46. Bandleader Les
47. Revolted
48. Not neat at the ends
50. More imminent
53. Pioneer in Cubism
55. Fido and friends
56. "___ recall . . ."
58. Take out
60. "Buddenbrooks" novelist Thomas
63. Surfing site
64. Big bird
65. Opposite SSW
66. Classic Jaguar

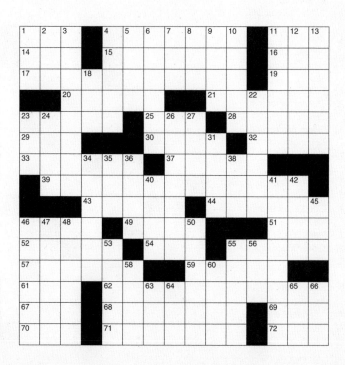

WHISKEY, YOU'RE THE DEVIL

by Fred Piscop

ACROSS

1. N.B.A.'s O'Neal, familiarly
5. Nicklaus's org.
8. Orbital point
13. Cape Canaveral grp.
14. E.T. vehicles
15. The Beatles' "You Won't ___"
16. Santa checks it twice
17. Popular adhesive
19. Facility
21. Egg ___ yung
22. And others: Abbr.
23. Canasta relative
26. Cash register key
28. ___ trick (three goals)
29. It kept a princess up
30. Dallas player, for short
31. Small island
32. "Oh, ___ kind of guy . . ."
34. Score in horseshoes
37. New Orleans hot spot
41. Edits
42. Overindulgent parent, e.g.
44. "Meet the Press" network
47. Actress Sue ___ Langdon
48. Feather source
50. ___-Magnon
51. Conditioning, as leather
53. Ham holder
55. Golfer's pocketful
56. Cool ___ cucumber
58. Future atty.'s exam
59. 1777 battle site
62. Worst possible score
65. Role player
66. Athlete with a statue in Richmond, Va.
67. Hydrox rival
68. Villa ___ (Italian site)
69. Hair goo
70. Highway entrance

DOWN

1. Variety show since 1975, briefly
2. "Bali ___"
3. O.K.
4. Persian Gulf nation
5. Army rank E-3
6. Disney star
7. Regarding
8. Campfire remnant
9. "For ___ sake!"
10. Washington State airport
11. Relative of a gazelle
12. Old vaudeville actress Blossom
14. 1972 Bill Withers hit
18. Longtime Harvard president James Bryant ___
20. Second-biggest movie hit of 1978
23. Touch-tone 4
24. Poetic foot
25. "Cheers" bar owner Sam
27. Recording studio add-ins
30. Raymond of "East of Eden"
33. Shade
35. Tackle's neighbor
36. Custom Royale of old autodom
38. Popular pain relief cream
39. And so on
40. Trillion: Prefix
43. Engine part
44. So-so
45. Writer Ambrose
46. Footballer's footwear
49. Free-for-all
52. "Once ___ Enough"
53. Pay boost
54. Shadow eliminator?
57. Booty
60. Rap's Dr. ___
61. Devils' org.
63. Dream period, for short
64. Alley ___

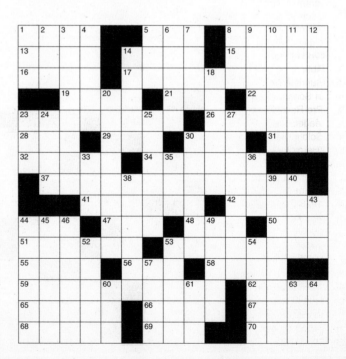

"HEY, BARTENDER"

by Elizabeth C. Gorski

ACROSS
1. Free ticket
5. Watercress unit
10. Throw off
14. Neighborhood
15. Fraternity ___
16. Fast feline
17. Cheery tune
18. Bewildered
19. Kind of rain
20. 1980 Neil Diamond hit
23. Yalie
24. Barker and Kettle, e.g.
25. "Siddhartha" author
27. ___-car
29. Injure
32. Nickname
33. Creature caught only by a virgin maiden
36. Prefix with -gramme
37. Secret competitor
40. Beam
41. Liqueur flavoring
42. Kind of stock: Abbr.
43. Sunrise direction, in Sonora
44. Pre-Revolution leaders
48. Solo in Berlioz's "Harold in Italy"
50. Daschle or Dodd: Abbr.
52. Formerly
53. 1978 Oscar-winning prison documentary
58. Pessimist's comments
59. Monastery figure
60. Rendezvous
61. Change for a ten
62. Argentine dance
63. Wings
64. About

65. Product of Bethlehem
66. Basketball's Archibald

DOWN
1. Telemarketer
2. Baltimore bird
3. Litigator Belli
4. Toast topping
5. Alexander, formerly of "60 Minutes"
6. "Designing Women" co-star
7. Hurry
8. Words of understanding
9. Trucker's choice
10. Part of NASA
11. Snake oil salesman
12. Go-between

13. June honoree
21. Saudi neighbor
22. Physicist Georg
26. Bruised item
28. Not go straight
29. Guts
30. Lincoln Center subject
31. Memo starter
34. Lupino and others
35. Copper
36. Tacks on
37. Masons, coopers and the like
38. Glance
39. Big insurance carrier
40. N.J.'s Whitman, e.g.
43. Pitcher part
45. Bassett of "Waiting to Exhale"

46. Warm up, as leftovers
47. Living room piece
49. Rancher's rope
50. Put on
51. Flynn of film
54. Newts
55. "Phooey!"
56. Kind of curve, in math
57. "___ old cowhand . . ."
58. Constrictor

BEHAVE YOURSELF

by William Bernhardt

ACROSS

1. One of 7-Down
6. Nicholas II, e.g.
10. Tattle
14. Kind of anesthetic
15. Roll call response
16. "I before E except after C," e.g.
17. Make amends
18. The witch's end in "Hansel and Gretel"
19. Where India is
20. Restorative
21. Former Attorney General Janet
22. Ollie's partner in slapstick
23. Popular oil additive
25. Tough as ___
27. One leads to Loch Lomond
31. Mounted again
35. Collection of anecdotes
36. One of 7-Down
38. Small drum
39. Signal for an act to end
41. Holy chalice of legend
43. Telephone sound
44. It increases by degrees
46. Make sense
48. The Red Baron was one
49. Curriculum vitae
51. Striped
53. Midsection, informally
55. It hangs next to 53-Across
56. "Hey, you!"
59. Growth on the north side of trees
61. Monastery staff
65. Reverberation

66. Satanic
67. 1973 Broadway revival starring Debbie Reynolds
68. Pour
69. Singer Turner
70. Gypsy's deck
71. One of 7-Down
72. Midterm, e.g.
73. One of 7-Down

DOWN

1. Subdivision of land
2. ___-Rooter
3. It's clicked on a computer
4. Breakfast pastry for Hamlet?
5. Sophocles tragedy
6. God with a hammer
7. This puzzle's theme
8. "In the___" (Nixon book)
9. Impressionist Pierre
10. High military muck-a-muck
11. One of 7-Down
12. Inter ___
13. Noggin
24. Ping-___
26. Serve to be reserved
27. Cartoon Viking
28. Hole-___
29. The Sharks and the Jets, e.g.
30. Taj Mahal site
32. German sub
33. Present
34. One of 7-Down
37. "___, Pagliacci" (aria)

40. One of 7-Down
42. Moon goddess
45. Grounded bird
47. Drivers and hunters need them
50. Clown Kelly
52. Not concerned with right and wrong
54. Hollywood release
56. Dumas senior
57. Glance over
58. Thug's knife
60. Blinds piece
62. Peter or the Wolfe?
63. Half hitch, e.g.
64. Brother of Cain and Abel

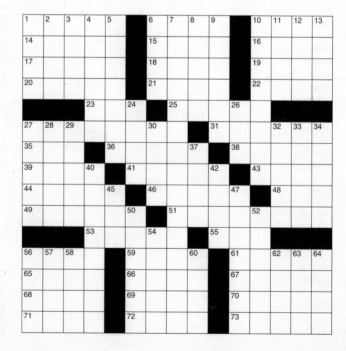

FOR SPEED SOLVERS ONLY

by Janet R. Bender

ACROSS

1. Poker holding
5. Study for finals
9. Shaping machine
14. "Crimes & Misdemeanors" actor
15. Wife of Zeus
16. Flynn of "Captain Blood"
17. Fast
20. Land, as a big one
21. Late Chairman
22. Blood supplies
23. Long, long time
25. Hall-of-Famer Drysdale
27. Swift
35. Didn't face the enemy
36. Chow down
37. Like a Jaguar or Miata
38. Was in a play
41. Ms. alternative
43. ___ raving mad
44. Deutsch, here
46. Swiss peak
48. Society page word
49. Fleet
53. Fat farm
54. Pouting face
55. "Dance On, Little Girl" singer
59. Piercing tool
61. Opera house cries
65. Quick
68. Non-earthling
69. Otherwise
70. ___ Stanley Gardner
71. Old-fashioned
72. Fate
73. Aussie hoppers

DOWN

1. Henry VIII's sixth
2. Not into the wind
3. Not in use
4. Criticize harshly
5. Hong Kong residents, now
6. ___ Speedwagon
7. Calla lily family
8. Symbol of Jewish resistance
9. Hawaiian garland
10. Fine or liberal follower
11. "How ___!"
12. Frost
13. Singer Fitzgerald
18. Best Picture of 1958
19. They may need coloring at a salon
24. Deception
26. Small bites
27. Fort ___, N.C.
28. Indy entrant
29. Prelim
30. Horse stall covering
31. Go bad
32. Neighbor of an Afghani
33. Sore throat cause, briefly
34. Little squirts, so to speak
39. Big bird
40. Drops bait
42. Brickbat
45. Like some stocks
47. Bit of math homework
50. Acted servilely
51. Hang ten or shoot the curl
52. Medicine man
55. In the distance
56. Aswan's river
57. Make an afghan
58. "Hard Hearted Hannah" composer
60. Composer Schifrin
62. ___ Beach, Fla.
63. Norse capital
64. Tom Jones's "___ a Lady"
66. Brian of rock music
67. Prefix with metric

56

HERE'S LOOKING AT YOU

by Elizabeth C. Gorski

ACROSS

1. "Shoo!"
5. Bishop of old TV
10. Like some furs
14. Forbidden: Var.
15. Ballroom dance
16. Novelist ___ S. Connell Jr.
17. Gobs
18. Sharon of Israel
19. Behind schedule
20. Righteous Brothers' musical style
23. Cool fabric
24. Crisp fabric
28. Coda's place in a score
29. House of ___
33. Thingamajig
34. Think about
36. Old-time actor Wallace ___
37. 1967 Van Morrison hit
41. Handel oratorio
42. Say again
43. Teamed up (with)
46. CD player maker
47. Corp. giant
50. They practice girth control
52. Less convincing, as an excuse
54. Popular Southern vegetable
58. Lima's locale
61. Sao ___
62. Touch down
63. 1934 Pulitzer writer Herbert
64. Church officer
65. "Or ___!"
66. Big Apple section
67. Logician in space
68. Sunbeams

DOWN

1. Place to start a ride
2. Check voicemail, perhaps
3. Be plentiful
4. Student
5. Judge's order
6. Fabled fast starter
7. Oklahoma city
8. Discharge
9. Type of mutual fund
10. Took the bait
11. One of Frank's exes
12. Krazy ___
13. Opposite WSW
21. Fund
22. Sky light?
25. German river
26. Peacock's pride
27. Supplement
30. Bed-and-breakfast
31. River through Frankfurt
32. Juan Carlos and others
34. Former Kremlin hotshots
35. Property taken back
37. Hope-Crosby's "Road to ___"
38. Govern
39. Hideout
40. Singer Crystal
41. Down
44. Sushi bar order
45. Window treatments
47. African antelope
48. Wee
49. Swaps
51. Resell at a profit
53. Philosopher Mortimer
55. Bit of praise
56. Util. bill
57. Duchess of ___
58. Dads
59. Kind of maniac
60. "Go, team!"

PEOPLE TELL ME . . .

by Stephanie Spadaccini

ACROSS

1. Dateless
5. Chitchat
9. Chorus voice
14. Pasty
15. Prince William's school
16. Cancel
17. "___ me."
20. Stop working
21. Pull a con
22. Clear tables and such
23. Where le nez is
25. Door opener
27. Do film work
30. Pillow cover
32. Coercion
36. Bikini tops
38. Provo neighbor
40. Medicine for what ails you
41. "___ me!"
44. Lethargy
45. Second of three virtues
46. Where to see a hula
47. Draw
49. Dick Francis book "Dead ___"
51. Make a mistake
52. Unopened
54. Porn
56. Nothing's alternative
59. "Phooey!"
61. Gets used (to)
65. "___ me?"
68. Eskimo boat
69. Christen
70. Suffix with billion
71. Stately place
72. Barks
73. Pig food

DOWN

1. Practice with Rocky
2. Saga
3. Got down
4. "Understand?"
5. TV money-raiser
6. Gobbled up
7. Passing shots
8. New York hoopster
9. Disparage
10. Hard-working insect
11. Snooty one
12. "Star Trek" character
13. Auto maker Ransom E. ___
18. Very, in Valence
19. Currency, in Capetown
24. "Planet of the Apes" planet
26. Range choice
27. Gaping pit
28. Bo-peep's staff
29. Brownish gray
31. French wine district
33. Follow
34. Sound of the 60's
35. Scrub
37. Glaswegians, e.g.
39. Is gloomy
42. Former Austrian prince
43. Home wreckers
48. Affronted
50. Star-Kist product
53. Lion-colored
55. Oompah instruments
56. Buzzing
57. Champagne Tony of golf
58. "___ Eyes" (Eagles hit)
60. Siamese, now
62. Stir up
63. Prefix with dollar or trash
64. Escalator part
66. ___-relief
67. Bit of electricity

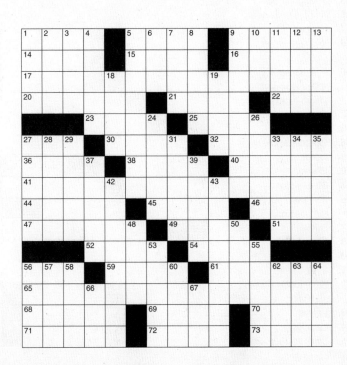

FEELING GREAT

by Alan Arbesfeld

ACROSS

1. "Red" tree
6. Tues., for Tuesday
10. Poland's Walesa
14. 24 sheets of paper
15. Peeved
16. First name in scat
17. Open, as a bottle
18. They produce a row on the farm
19. Swear
20. "Act your ___!"
21. Elated
24. Opera set in the time of the Pharaohs
25. Hershey brand
26. Elated
31. Handy
32. Large pitcher
33. Triangular sail
36. Fall cleanup need
37. Longed
39. Western writer Grey
40. P, in Greece
41. "Hi-___, Hi-Lo" (1953 film song)
42. Quarterback Brett
43. Elated
46. Countenance
49. Open
50. Elated
53. 33 or 45, e.g.
56. It's taken out at the seams
57. Bucket
58. "Behold!"
60. Writer Lindbergh
61. Ever
62. Ballyhooed sitcom of 1997
63. Latvian
64. Lack
65. Chill, so to speak

DOWN

1. Shade of blue
2. It's breath-taking
3. Cut into cubes
4. Stat for Maddux
5. Dinosaur, e.g.
6. Depth charge, in slang
7. Engage, as an entertainer
8. Belgian songwriter Jacques
9. Not showing emotions
10. Ballet dancer, at times
11. Oft-cited sighting
12. Copy
13. Peddles
22. Uganda's Amin
23. Forest denizen
24. Competent
26. Extra-short haircut
27. Bryce Canyon locale
28. Anti-apartheid activist Steven
29. Magic wish granters
30. Be in debt
33. Cawfee
34. Letters for Jesus
35. Miller, for one
37. Join in a football heap
38. Kind
39. Wacky
41. Italy's ___ di Como
42. Eternally
43. Picture gallery site?
44. Threw out, as a runner
45. Word to end a card game
46. Song part
47. Hole-___
48. Meager
51. Scandinavian
52. Enjoyable
53. Brook
54. Emotional request
55. Domestic cat
59. Corrida cry

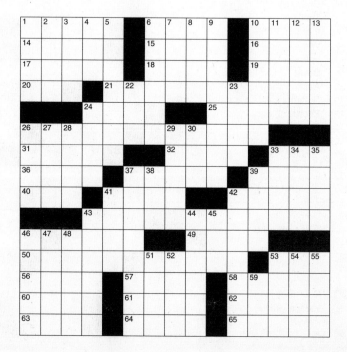

TASTE TEST

by Elizabeth C. Gorski

ACROSS

1. Fruit of the Loom rival
6. Where boys will be boys
10. Frost
14. Word with time or rights
15. Indian music
16. Some mutual fund accts.
17. Ingratiate oneself, e.g.
19. Dust busters, for short
20. Film critic Pauline
21. Cuckoo bird
22. Style
23. Original state
27. "Virginia Woolf" dramatist
29. 1955 children's heroine
30. Ogle
32. Charged particle
33. Mail carriers have them: Abbr.
37. With 6-Down, operator of a 63-Down
38. Auction offering
40. Butterfly catcher
42. Pitcherful, maybe
43. Droops
45. Post–W.W. II grp.
47. "Shucks!"
49. La Scala productions
52. Shark watchers' protectors
53. Sherlock Holmes player
57. Way in
58. Sale item marking: Abbr.
59. Big exam
62. Pulitzer writer James
63. Words of wisdom

66. "Twittering Machine" artist
67. Gulf war missile
68. Al __ (firm)
69. Does lawn work
70. Summer shirts
71. Lock of hair

DOWN

1. "Shucks!"
2. Water color
3. Famed trial venue
4. Before now
5. Like Wile E. Coyote
6. See 37-Across
7. Italian cheese or meat dish
8. Give it __ (try)
9. Roof top
10. Rosie the __
11. Khomeini, for one
12. Computer shortcut
13. German Pittsburgh
18. The 2% of 2%
22. Dogfaces, today
24. Patricia of "Hud"
25. Twelve __
26. Ate fancily
27. Word of resignation
28. "Star Wars" princess
31. Radio station need
34. Cousin of an orange
35. Peace Nobelist Wiesel
36. Places for props
39. "Gone With the Wind" setting
41. Guacamole's place
44. Evening get-togethers

46. Rundown feeling
48. Hurried next door, e.g.
50. Thickness
51. Tears up
53. Prominent toucan features
54. The "A" of WASP
55. Riding horse
56. Stagewear for Madonna
60. Plays the part
61. Some popular jeans
63. See 37-Across
64. Serve like Sampras, e.g.
65. Banned pesticide

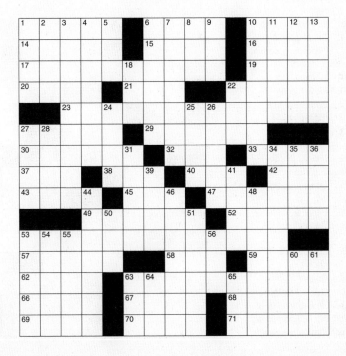

VERY SCARY

by Christopher Page

ACROSS

1. "Holy mackerel!"
5. Shady lady
9. Landscaper's tool
14. California wine valley
15. 1847 South Seas adventure
16. Running bowline, e.g.
17. Desert mount
19. 7–11 game
20. Full up
21. Aria, usually
23. "j" topper
24. "Yuck!"
25. Place for marbles
29. Baby blues
31. Hillbilly TV fare
35. Strait of Dover port
37. Got some shuteye
38. Hightail it
40. New Zealand native
43. Executive: Abbr.
44. Bit of parsley
46. "You've got my support"
48. Settles bills
50. How many bouquets are made
53. Desperation football pass
56. Native: Suffix
57. Bad Ems, e.g.
60. School sports org.
61. Gave a ticket
63. Caterpillar, for one
65. Irish locale of song
68. Caper
69. Go ___ detail
70. "The Masque of Alfred" composer
71. Kind of answer
72. Kind of tide
73. Humorist Bill and others

DOWN

1. Finishes
2. Home annex
3. Rx purveyor
4. Woman of distinction
5. Physique, slangily
6. Physicians' grp.
7. "What's the ___ that could happen?"
8. "___ mind?"
9. They follow standing ovations
10. Golden, in France
11. Spur
12. Hockey great Phil, familiarly
13. Take five
18. 1957 Ford debut
22. ___-di-dah
26. Bygone London transport
27. Part of SEATO
28. Barker
30. Reverend's responsibility
32. Like many titles
33. "Tarzan" extra
34. Lb. and kg.
36. ___-distant (self styled): Fr.
38. Recipe amt.
39. Emissions tester: Abbr.
41. Pro___
42. Operatic prince
45. Camel's cousin
47. Rolls's partner
49. Paparazzo's prize
51. Ev'rlasting
52. Goes brunette this time
54. "E pluribus unum," e.g.
55. Bath's state
57. Leave laughing
58. Glazier's unit
59. Theater, opera, etc.
62. Tabriz's land
64. Bordeaux, e.g.
66. Educ. group
67. Top 40 music

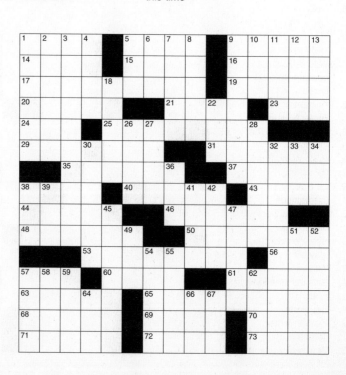

JUNK FOOD?

61

Nancy Salomon

ACROSS

1. Catherine who survived Henry VIII
5. Eden dweller
9. ___-ski
14. Theater award
15. Timber wolf
16. Fit to be tied
17. Dieter's credo?
19. One of Lear's daughters
20. French farewell
21. Program airing
23. State of high alarm
26. Praiseful poem
27. Dieter's credo?
32. Pitcher's pride
35. First name in scat
36. Flood embankment
37. Hi-jinks in a stolen car
40. Determines limits in advance
42. Had title to
43. Regarding
45. Realize
46. Dieter's credo?
50. Calamity
51. Comic musical work
55. Mt. Rainier's site, with "the"
59. "___ Pretty" (song for Maria)
60. Anticipate
61. Dieter's credo?
64. It results from work well done
65. Gamblers' mecca
66. This, in Mexico
67. Polk's predecessor
68. Dutch cheese
69. Bygone Tunisian V.I.P.'s

DOWN

1. Kind of bear
2. Stand for
3. Unbending
4. Fix, as leftovers
5. Draught, maybe
6. Mafia boss
7. Act of touching
8. Wear a long face
9. Terrier type
10. Comes before
11. Indian music style
12. Greek H's
13. On its way, as a message
18. Noted site of ancient Mexican ruins
22. British john
24. Managed, with "out"
25. Take the reins again
28. Portable PC
29. Place to broil
30. Lavish party
31. Suffix with gab or slug
32. "Get ___" (1958 hit)
33. English poet laureate Nicholas
34. Popular pet bird
38. Killing of a king
39. Blind worshiper
41. Banned Pete
44. Stinko
47. Like the gray mare
48. Actor Estrada
49. Officiated a game
52. Rib
53. Irascible
54. Choir voices
55. Nemo, e.g.: Abbr.
56. Not straight
57. Leave dock
58. To be, in France
62. One-million link
63. ___ de guerre

PITCH-ERS?

62

Nancy Schuster

ACROSS

1. Follower of Mary
5. Return to base before proceeding
10. Hot springs
13. Resort town near Santa Barbara
14. "You ___ Beautiful" (1975 Joe Cocker hit)
15. Hard to comprehend
16. Sneaky thief
18. Flying-related
19. Mined metal
20. Real howler
21. In shreds
23. Dagger handle
24. Close
25. In ___ (intrinsically)
28. Comedy brothers of 60's–70's TV
32. Satirist Mort
33. Set in "Die Fledermaus"
34. Prez's stand-in
35. Skater's maneuver
36. ___ Carlo
37. Spanish general Duke of ___
38. A very good pair
39. Egyptian cross
40. Cherished
41. Bargain with the prosecutor
43. Jumpy
45. Signals at Sotheby's
46. Item on a cowboy boot
47. Slightly bounce
50. "Pardon me"
51. Draft org.
54. Double-reed instrument
55. Theme of this puzzle
58. Ship's spine
59. Chrissie of tennis
60. Jai ___
61. U.F.O. crew
62. Old yet new again
63. Toasty

DOWN

1. Nuts or crackers
2. Slightly open
3. Aussie buddy
4. It's usually served with lobster
5. Import duty
6. Shoptalk
7. Moolah
8. It's a free country
9. Window onto the ocean
10. Caught sight of
11. Lima's land
12. Each
15. Luke Skywalker's father
17. Russia's ___ Mountains
22. Not at home
23. Member of a notorious biker gang
24. Will of 55-Across
25. Writer Asimov
26. Tourist mecca near Mexico City
27. Blind followers
28. The daddy of decafs
29. Went congering
30. Pack again, as groceries
31. Fifth wheel
33. Tommy Lee of 55-Across
36. Seagoer's woe
42. Campaigner, for short
43. Not rejecting out of hand
44. Not feeling
46. Bake, as eggs
47. Speechmaker's opening
48. "Yeah, sure!"
49. Proceeds
50. Work without ___ (be daring)
51. Hacienda room
52. Wound reminder
53. Dairy-case choice
56. Adam's mate
57. Jurisprudence

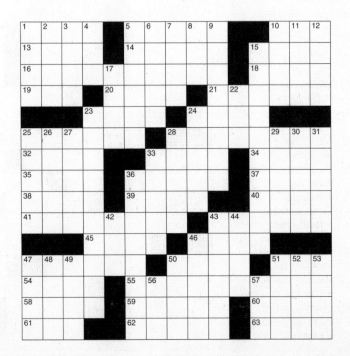

SINGULAR VISION

Richard Hughes

ACROSS

1. Kind of layer
6. Applaud
10. Locking device
14. Of neap and ebb
15. Overconfident racer of fable
16. Charles Lamb pseudonym
17. Raise
18. Quickly, quickly
19. Charitable donation
20. Start of a Daniel Webster quote
22. "Act now!"
23. New England's Cape ___
24. Generally
26. Turn to cinders
29. Sentry's cry
32. Prevent from acting
33. Chicken ___
34. Syrup brand
35. Radical college org.
36. Middle of the quote
42. California's Fort ___
43. Cover for a diamond
44. Theater sign
45. Élève's place
48. Janet of Justice
49. Latin love
50. Whom Reagan beat in 1984
52. Tanner's tub
54. Tweed, for one
55. End of the quote
61. Related
62. Andes land
63. Sporty Toyota
64. Rudner of comedy
65. Protection: Var.
66. Diet guru Jenny
67. Hang onto

68. Gusto
69. Refuges, old-style

DOWN

1. Roman emperor after Galba
2. Utah national park
3. Garfield's foil
4. Racing org.
5. Singer John
6. Honolulu-based detective
7. Survive
8. Noah's landfall
9. English diarist Samuel
10. Whiplash preventer
11. Total
12. Cousin of a metaphor
13. Scrapbook user

21. "___ me, villain!"
25. Total
26. Navy noncom
27. Sweetie
28. It's swung in forests
30. "___ longa, vita brevis"
31. Singer Lenya
34. "M*A*S*H" setting
35. Endeavored
37. Sudden arrival of fall weather
38. Author Fleming
39. Belief
40. Spanish gold
41. Negative joiner
45. Set sail
46. Gingersnap, e.g.
47. Kind of inspection
48. Go back on a promise
49. Rose oils

51. "If I Had a Hammer" singer
53. Pet protection org.
56. Goddess of discord
57. Problem for Sneezy?
58. "Do as ___, . . ."
59. Buzz's moonmate
60. Eastern discipline

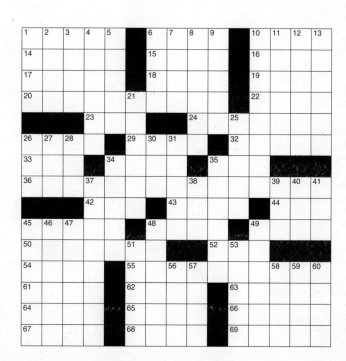

CATCH PHRASES

64

Robert Malinow

ACROSS

1. Struck, old-style
5. Uneven hairdo
9. Winery in Modesto, Calif.
14. Yesterday's dinner today
15. Smog
16. To no ___ (futilely)
17. Actor John, once married to Shirley Temple
18. Appliance on a board
19. Greene of "Bonanza"
20. "The Lone Ranger" catch phrase
23. Carryall
24. "Eureka!"
25. "The Honeymooners" catch phrase
32. Monte ___
33. Filleted fish
34. One with filling work?: Abbr.
35. Woodwind
36. Ground grain
38. Big elephant features
39. Announcer Pardo
40. Chimney duct
41. "God bless" preceder
42. "The Goldbergs" catch phrase
46. Spanish gold
47. Rebellious one, maybe
48. "Star Trek" catch phrase
55. In concealment
56. Report cards' stats
57. Pained look
58. Writer Nin
59. Needle case

60. College in New Rochelle
61. Whom Jason jilted
62. Part to play
63. Hatfields or McCoys, e.g.

DOWN

1. ___ of Iran
2. Travelers to Bethlehem
3. "___, old chap!"
4. Choke
5. Many an Iranian
6. Home of poet Langston Hughes
7. Asia's Sea of ___
8. Trait carrier
9. Lancelot's son
10. Promise
11. Zhivago's love
12. Streaked
13. Matador's cheer
21. It borders Regent Street
22. Charged
25. Pork, to a Jew, e.g.
26. Maine campus town
27. Willow
28. Circus cries
29. Popular potato
30. Modern "book"
31. Where an Edsel filled up, maybe
32. Wild West Show star
36. Despondency
37. ___ and Coke
38. Business-related
40. Where Taipei is
41. One of the Baldwins
43. Grinder

44. State capital on the Mississippi
45. Singer Smith
48. Rib, for one
49. "Heavens to Betsy!"
50. Elbe tributary
51. ___ no good
52. Cat's-paw
53. Cape Cod catch
54. Bear young, as sheep
55. Beaver's work

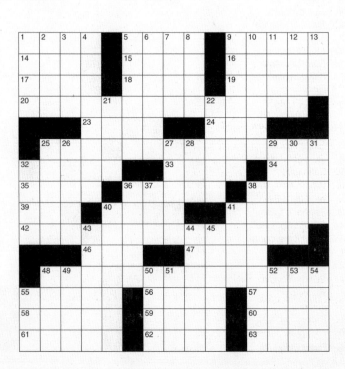

CLOTHES DO MAKE THE MEN

by Elizabeth C. Gorski

ACROSS

1. Like fine wine
5. Revival shouts
10. Impertinent one
14. Where the Vatican is
15. Newspapers, TV, etc.
16. Actress Petty
17. Suffix with psych- or neur-
18. Like a snake-oil salesman
19. Components of elevens
20. Aristocratic types
23. Berlioz's "Les nuits d'___"
24. Contained, with "up"
25. Packs down
28. Isn't feeling good
29. Dolt
31. Brink
33. Conquistador's haul
34. E or G, e.g.
35. Self-righteously virtuous types
40. Work unit
41. Start of many naval vessel names
42. Subject to breezes
43. Phrase in a new way, as a question
46. Throw hard
48. Farm mudholes
49. Salespeople, informally
50. Sheepish reply
53. Pompous types
57. Deep laugh
59. Vassal
60. Mata ___
61. Nondairy topping
62. Get-go
63. Former sneaker brand
64. Something to do
65. Uproots?
66. Campus figure

DOWN

1. Stood
2. "I understand!"
3. Classic Rousseau novel
4. Clobber
5. Popular brew from Holland
6. Cantaloupes
7. Proclamation
8. Shaving cut
9. Noted short-story writer
10. "Just say no," for instance
11. Favorable life insurance category
12. Miff
13. Detectives, for short
21. Used binoculars, maybe
22. To the ___ degree

26. Where "e'en" is seen
27. Heaven
28. Long ___
29. Full house sign
30. Beloved comic's nickname
31. White heron
32. Small sharks
33. Cries of pain
36. "Tasty!"
37. Mao ___-tung
38. Draconian
39. Van Gogh's "Irises," e.g.
40. Hesitant sounds
44. Shot again, as a photo
45. Tempe sch.
46. Didn't give a definite answer
47. Unexpected wins
49. Singer Della
50. Intrepid

51. Courtyards
52. Kind of flu
54. Move like lava
55. Better than good
56. "___ the Craziest Dream" (1942 song)
57. Steamy
58. Ending with schnozz

ALL ABOARD

by Bernice Gordon

ACROSS
1. Lots
5. Desert streambed
9. Tennis great Rod
14. "Are you some kind of ___?"
15. Black
16. "___ at the office"
17. Vidal's Breckinridge
18. Roar at the shore
19. Count with an orchestra
20. 1989 Madonna hit
23. Churchill's sign
24. Basic college degrees
25. Summit
29. ___-Jo (1988 Olympics name)
31. Mosque V.I.P.
35. Live, in a TV studio
36. Like Britain
38. Poetic palindrome
39. It may be used in minor surgery
42. Quattro minus uno
43. Freshman, sophomore, etc.
44. Revolving machine part
45. Reply to "Are not!"
47. 1–80, e.g.: Abbr.
48. Item in a Mexican fiesta
49. Luau dish
51. Sound from Sandy
52. Bibliophile's treasures
61. Belief in sorcery and magic
62. Pre-tractor farmer's need
63. Plummet
64. "A votre ___!"

65. Grp. affecting gas prices
66. Go gently (into)
67. More correct
68. Brood
69. "Jeopardy!" host Trebek

DOWN
1. Charades, e.g.
2. Cameo stone
3. Pat on the back, as a baby
4. Asterisk
5. Setting for Thomas Hardy novels
6. Maltreatment
7. Boat with oars
8. Data
9. Astrologically, the thoughtful, diplomatic type
10. Tennis great Andre
11. Bouquet site
12. Satanicalness
13. Sailor's peril
21. Don or Phil of 50's–60's pop
22. W.W. II menace
25. Physicist Alessandro
26. Vast, old-style
27. Regattas
28. Spanish aunt
29. French brother
30. Minus
32. Acclaimed "Hostess with the Mostes'"
33. Unrestrained
34. Stiller's comedy partner
36. Buzzing pest
37. Savings and loan

40. Condor's home
41. Long time
46. Narcotic
48. William or Harry, e.g.
50. Word with woman or worldly
51. Take ___ breath
52. Bewildered
53. Construction support
54. Maître d's offering
55. Condemn
56. Montreal player
57. Bright thought
58. Spoken
59. Winning margin, maybe
60. Glasses, in ads

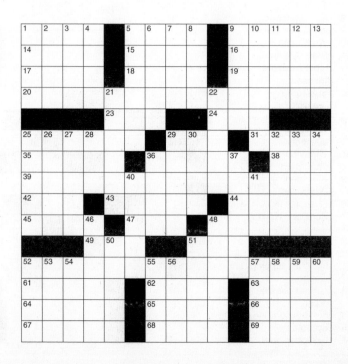

METROPOLITAN MUSIC

by Thomas W. Schier

ACROSS
1. Shopaholic's hangout
5. Out-and-out
10. Way to go
14. Pacific Rim locale
15. Shoe material
16. As a result
17. Part of a popular song lyric
20. Actress-skater Sonja
21. Chinese restaurant flowers
22. Suffix with idiom
25. Open, as an envelope
26. Old-fashioned illumination
30. Monticello, for one
34. 1970's discipline
35. Bête ___
37. Book after Gen.
38. More of the song's lyric
42. Do-well starter
43. Anteater's feature
44. Actress Peeples
45. Not asea
48. Supporters of Ivan and Nicholas
50. Sells (for)
52. Onetime Spanish queen and namesakes
53. Draws
57. Midafternoon
61. Statement describing the subject of the song
64. Nectar flavor
65. Microwave brand
66. Gave the boot
67. Censor's target
68. Where Durban is
69. Baseball's Sandberg

DOWN
1. It takes figuring
2. U.S. Open stadium name
3. Property encumbrance
4. Of the lips
5. G.I. entertainment grp.
6. Large cask
7. Sermon basis
8. Newswoman Magnus et al.
9. Secondhand transaction
10. Did a horticulturist's job
11. Planets and such
12. Malarial fever
13. Children's connectibles
18. Eye layer
19. "Trinity" author
23. "___ a Name" (Jim Croce hit)
24. Debt markers
26. "I can't ___ satisfaction" (1965 lyric)
27. Visibly frightened
28. Shipment to Detroit
29. E. C. Bentley detective
31. Impulse transmitters
32. Namely
33. Author Ferber and others
36. Jagged
39. Exaggerator
40. Chinese dollar
41. Geologic layers
46. One noted for bringing couples together
47. Abase
49. Babylonian love goddess
51. 1965 march site
53. Rewards for waiting
54. News bit
55. Son of Rebekah
56. Mattress support
58. Classic theater name
59. Gershwin biographer David
60. "Momo" author Michael
62. Actress Merkel
63. Actor Kilmer

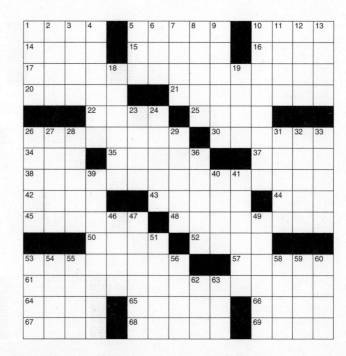

GO TO PIECES

by Brendan Emmett Quigley

ACROSS

1. ___ de Boulogne (Paris park)
5. Constant complainer
9. Excite, as interest
14. Ancient inscription
15. Daughter of Cronus
16. Pluck
17. Start with boy or girl
18. "The jig ___!"
19. Much-played part of a 45
20. Led Zeppelin hit, 1969
23. English ___
24. Rocker Garcia, informally
25. Big Blue
26. "___ Yes!" (old political placard)
28. Jewel
30. Classic clown
32. It comes after Mardi
33. Gagging cry
35. Actor Beatty
36. Make out
37. Midgame broadcasts
42. Inch, e.g.
43. "Pish posh!"
44. Part of an academic yr.
45. Sicilian spouter
46. McDonald's founder Ray
48. Dance version of a pop song, e.g.
52. "Comprende?"
53. Clump
54. Make sense, with "up"
56. British verb ending
57. Alternative to a Whopper
61. Deceit
62. Engagement gift
63. Waters: Fr.
64. Part of a furniture joint
65. Pins and needles holder
66. Fair distance
67. Works with words
68. Do carbon-testing on
69. Table scraps

DOWN

1. Barroom fights
2. Do better than at bat
3. Altogether
4. Whiskered circus animal
5. Its capital is Santiago
6. Soak up again
7. In ___ (stuck)
8. Saint John, for one
9. Sacred song
10. ___ facto
11. Shaker
12. Just walk through a role, say
13. Stretch, with "out"
21. Cassette deck button
22. Homes
27. Questions
29. First-term Clinton victory
31. ". . . and ___ grow on"
32. Treasure-hoarding dwarf
34. Popular candy bar
37. Tinted
38. Artificially made to look old
39. Pasta favorite
40. Trounced, in sports
41. Hidden
47. Screw backer
49. Any point in a trapeze artist's routine
50. Tristram's love
51. Persian king who destroyed Athens
53. Brown songbirds
55. Cowboy's stray
58. Tons
59. Meter maid of song
60. Verne captain
61. AT&T competitor

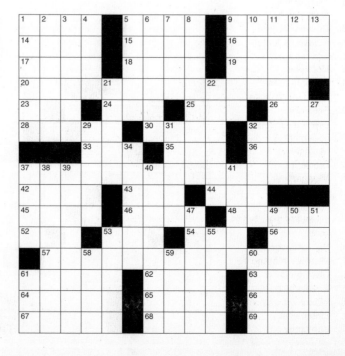

SIGNS OF A FREQUENT FLIER?

by Peter Gordon

ACROSS

1. Golf hazard
5. Abound
9. A few
13. ___ law (old Germanic legal code)
15. Lunchbox treat
16. Opposite of unter
17. Having feet pointing inward
19. Physics calculation
20. "Tender ___" (1983 Robert Duvall film)
21. "Holy smokes!"
23. Surfing site
24. Dutch airline
25. Not much for mixing
27. Attire
29. Onetime Yugoslav chief
30. The time of one's life
31. Brenda of the comics
32. Markets
33. Bewitch
34. Having keen vision
37. Baby beagle
40. Nonliteral humor
41. Dusk to dawn
45. 34th Prez
46. New Jersey hoopsters
47. Indian homes
48. Soup dishes
50. PC alternative
51. Home planet in a 1978–82 sitcom
52. One of the McCartneys
53. Dairy workers
55. Cinergy Field team
56. Like one's fun house mirror image, maybe
59. Baseball's Moises
60. Salinger dedicatee
61. Lace place mat
62. Journalist Hamill
63. Arousing
64. Protected

DOWN

1. Recipe amt.
2. Attire
3. Search for the unknown?
4. Jetty
5. Pole on a reservation
6. God of love
7. Very wide, shoewise
8. In a humble way
9. Poison ___
10. Book after Amos
11. Bit of E-mail
12. Hosp. areas
14. Foolish
18. Cairo's river
22. Flexible, like some lamp shafts
23. "Scream" director Craven
25. Choreographer Alvin
26. Big Apple subway stop, for short
28. Mine metal
29. Rebellious time
32. Casino machines
35. Soldiers' "pineapples"
36. Quick swim
37. Raucous card game
38. Tiny Tim's instrument
39. August birthstone
42. Where Athens is
43. Feminine pronoun
44. "Naughty, naughty!"
47. Like most N.B.A. players
49. Follow
50. Boy in Life cereal ads
53. 1910, on cornerstones
54. Stars have big ones
55. Hip-hop
57. Put to work
58. Hair coloring

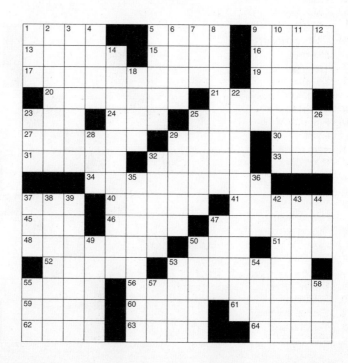

WHERE I COME FROM

by Gregory E. Paul

ACROSS

1. Handle the situation
5. Harbinger
9. Pancake topper
14. Drifters' "___ the Roof"
15. Application form information
16. Monopoly purchase
17. Alex Raymond comic strip
19. Peter of Peter and Gordon
20. C.I.A. forerunner
21. Tokyo, once
22. Coin side
24. Feature of five U.S. Presidents
26. Apollo vehicle
27. Manager Anderson
30. Following orders
35. Corporate emblems
36. Clumsy dancer's problems
37. The Magi, e.g.
38. Christie or Quindlen
39. Things to crack
40. Part of E.M.T.: Abbr.
41. Kind of tea
42. Pearl Buck heroine
43. Sacred song
44. Western Hemisphere
46. Sliding dance step
47. The Red Baron, for one
48. Curtain fabric
50. Musicians
54. Electric swimmer
55. Telephonic 3
58. Kind of board

59. Legendary cowboy
62. Attach to a lapel
63. Wicked
64. Come in last
65. Adlai's 1956 running mate
66. Broad valley
67. Sloth's home

DOWN

1. Stephen King novel
2. Musical composition
3. Operatic Lily
4. H.S. course
5. "Sometime . . ."
6. Captain's superior
7. Record label with Capitol
8. Commander of the Nautilus

9. Attacked the whiskers
10. Ornery Warner Bros. cartoon character
11. Essen's river
12. Manipulates
13. Father, in France
18. Vichyssoise ingredients
23. Give a benediction
24. Namath's nickname
25. Gadgets
27. Done in
28. Puerto Rican port city
29. 1973 resigner
31. Existed
32. Humorist Bombeck et al.
33. Physicist Bohr

34. The Velvet Fog
36. Bridge fee
39. Kitchen utensil
43. Collins and Donahue
45. Seas
46. Louisiana lingo
49. Heavy-hitting Fielder
50. "Essay on Man" author
51. San ___ Obispo, Calif.
52. "You ___ seen nothin' yet!"
53. Raced
55. New Look designer
56. If not
57. Head for the hills
60. Stowe girl
61. Lunch order, briefly

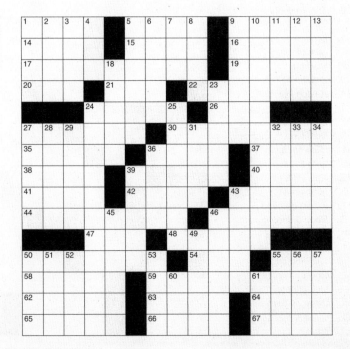

TIME TO WORK ONE'S TAIL OFF

by Alan Olschwang

ACROSS

1. Half of a 60's quartet
6. Small farm spread
10. Explorer Vasco da ___
14. Necklace fastener
15. Linseed oil source
16. Caboose
17. Alaska's first capital
18. Freeway exit
19. ___ the Red
20. Start of a quote by Lily Tomlin
23. Twosome
24. Chimney accumulation
25. "What ___ the odds?"
26. Graze
29. Moo
31. Engaged in swordplay
33. Part 2 of the quote
37. Overfill
38. Swift bird
39. Verdi heroine
43. Part 3 of the quote
48. Slug but good
51. Dandy
52. Select, with "for"
53. Coach Parseghian
54. Tabularize
57. Dorothy Parker quality
59. End of the quote
64. Fishing item
65. A beret covers it
66. Garden bulb
68. Sailing
69. "Symphonie Espagnole" composer
70. $C_4H_8O_2$, e.g.
71. Canine cry
72. Utopia
73. "Hansel and Gretel," for one

DOWN

1. Compaq products
2. Came down to earth
3. Way
4. Popped a question
5. Flipper?
6. 60's haircut
7. North Pole name
8. Stallone title role
9. Detonate
10. Matured
11. Kind of photo
12. ___ d'hôtel
13. Like a gateway, often
21. 2, to 4 or 8
22. Needle case
26. U.F.O. crew
27. "Yes, I see!"
28. ___ offensive
30. Birdhouse resident
32. Jacob's twin
34. Lively old dance
35. Paris associate
36. Sleeve's end
40. ___ Jima
41. Immerse
42. Tiny worker
44. Mouselike animal
45. Letter
46. Cry of pain
47. Tranquilizers
48. Attack en route
49. Impassion
50. Victor's prize
55. Ending with farm or home
56. Library info
58. Kind of account
60. Harvest
61. Revolutionary Trotsky
62. Countertenor
63. Stadium section
67. Meddle

A LITTLE NIGHT MUSIC

Fran and Lou Sabin

ACROSS

1. Pea holders
5. Coagulate
9. Not bold
14. Declare
15. Frost
16. "Swan Lake" maiden
17. Stupefy
18. Moffo at the Met
19. Nice ___ (prudish one)
20. Popular sing-along tune of 1925
23. Whiz
24. Picked at, picked at, picked at
27. Hubbub
30. Fill with feeling
34. Literary inits.
35. Minor dents
37. What a chapeau covers
38. Art Deco pioneer
39. 1954 song with a repeating title
42. "O.K., why not?"
43. Bagel or bialy
44. Type type
45. Prefix with sphere or disaster
46. Visits
48. Kind of school
49. Clog
51. ___ minérale
53. 1954 #1 hit by the Chordettes
60. Meager
62. Foolish fellow
63. Mustachioed artist
64. Postal scale unit
65. Revolutionary hero Nathan
66. Prez
67. Beautician's device
68. Scent
69. "Casablanca" role

DOWN

1. Goalie gear
2. Face's shape, approximately
3. Nap
4. Win all the games
5. One of a set of 64, maybe
6. Fluff
7. Home of the Hawks, with "the"
8. Hawks or Seahawks, e.g.
9. Deli meat offering
10. Notions
11. Grain grinder's power source
12. ___-timed
13. Actress Susan
21. Color separator
22. Violinist Zimbalist
25. Home in the country
26. Considered
27. Confounds
28. Run the show
29. Drinker's excess
31. Sen. Thurmond
32. "The Old Wives' Tale" dramatist
33. Biased writing?: Abbr.
36. Bromo target
38. Bit of work
40. Let fall, in poetry
41. Israel's Moshe
46. General called "Yellowhair"
47. Kitchen gadget
50. ___-nez
52. Milk source
54. Hollow reply?
55. Way to go
56. Fly like Lindy
57. 60's–70's dress
58. Novelist Waugh
59. Shaver's woe
60. Green cover
61. Junkyard dog

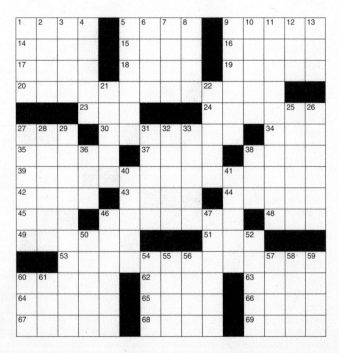

PARTNERS IN RHYME

by Elizabeth C. Gorski

ACROSS

1. They welcome people at the door
5. Gymnast Korbut
9. Lariat
14. Carrier to Jerusalem
15. News "items"
16. ___ Island (immigrants' spot)
17. Turkish title
18. "Inventions of the Monsters" artist
19. German currency, informally
20. Mother of country music
22. "___ Johnny!"
23. Takes care of
24. River to the Fulda
26. Alpine transport
29. Not just
33. Cousin of a stogie
37. Colorless
39. Arm bone
40. Prefix with mechanics
41. Tasmanian ___
42. Bonkers
43. Caroled
44. "Got you"
45. Fernando's farewell
46. Famous last words?
48. Garage job
50. Cheer (for)
52. Lawrence's land
57. Eastern mystic
60. Melville hero
63. "The Rebel" essayist
64. Romantic interlude
65. Out of port
66. Positive pole
67. Singer Horne
68. Cross-check
69. Types wearing pocket protectors
70. Extend credit
71. Point on Columbus's compass

DOWN

1. Stands for
2. Lake life
3. Western resort
4. Shuts vehemently
5. Handyman's assignment
6. Molokai meal
7. Like some charge cards
8. "All kidding ___ . . ."
9. "Little" storybook character
10. Cartoon character with a big gun
11. Agricultural chemical
12. Enervate
13. Entreats
21. "Tell ___ the Marines!"
25. One-on-one
27. Copies
28. Get tangled up
30. Jai ___
31. Data
32. Lab runners
33. Ski resort legwear?
34. Wife of Jacob
35. Composer Thomas
36. Onetime CBS anchor
38. Stead
41. Purcell's "___ and Aeneas"
45. Hawk's home: Var.
47. Boom and zoom
49. "Ode to Billie Joe," e.g.
51. Govt. security
53. Drop off
54. Double-deckers, e.g.
55. That is
56. "___which will live in infamy": F.D.R.
57. Glance over
58. Drop off
59. Love overseas
61. Concept for Claudette
62. Newswoman Sherr

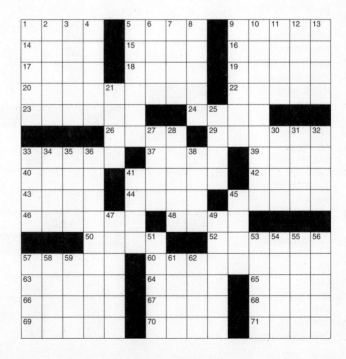

LOTS

by Fred Piscop

ACROSS

1. Islands west of Portugal
7. Third place
11. Southern ___
14. Barrio grocery
15. Hardly believable
16. "You ___ here"
17. Diane Keaton, to Woody Allen, often
18. Author Turgenev
19. Arrangement of masts
20. Lots, pricewise
23. H. H. Munro, pseudonymously
26. Velvet finish
27. Effortless
28. Ike of the O.K. Corral
31. Priestly garb
34. Josh
35. The Four Seasons' "Walk Like ___"
37. Coffee shop emanations
41. Lots, lovewise
44. Make some after-the-whistle contact
45. Dutch portraitist Frans
46. Fri. preceder
47. Sabbath activity
49. Deck out
51. Jump out of one's skin?
54. Dine
56. Chess castle
57. Lots, timewise
62. Boxers' letters?
63. Bowser's bowlful
64. Ducks
68. Brain scan, for short
69. Boo-boo
70. Chewy confection
71. High-pH substance
72. Dog's breath
73. Cleopatra's love

DOWN

1. "20/20" network
2. Where to do some petting
3. Takes too much
4. Hire, as counsel
5. Richard of "A Summer Place"
6. Franklin D.'s mother
7. Gunk
8. Harbor where the Maine blew up
9. Mideast land
10. Proceed
11. "Cheers" waitress
12. 80's Dodge
13. Having attractive gams
21. Of the kidneys
22. Ancient moralist
23. Dump into a Dumpster
24. "I ran out of gas," e.g.
25. Afghan capital
29. Sierra Nevada lake
30. Future signs
32. Serve, as stew
33. Chutzpah
36. Slangy refusal
38. Copycat's words
39. Allergy season sound
40. ___ cabbage
42. Sealy rival
43. 1993 treaty, briefly
48. Tough pickup for some bowlers
50. Audition
51. Old-time actress Normand
52. Hand-wringer's words
53. Rock shelf
55. Vote to accept
58. Heavy file
59. Milan's Teatro ___ Scala
60. "Two Years Before the Mast" writer
61. (Ding-dong) "___ calling"
65. Billy Joel's "___ to Extremes"
66. Dapper fellow?
67. Piggery

FAITHFUL FOLKS

by Elizabeth C. Gorski

ACROSS

1. Teeny amounts
5. ___ nova
10. Japanese middle managers?
14. Metallurgists' studies
15. Perfume
16. Zippo
17. Meanie
18. Old TV comic
20. Blonde's secret, maybe
21. Ladies' man
22. Memorable name
24. Holier-than-thou type
28. Set boundaries
31. Some soda pops
32. Compunction
36. Lyric poem
37. "The Dunciad" writer
41. Latin lady: Abbr.
42. Keeps from escaping
43. Zhou ___
46. They show the way
50. Hip characters
54. "___ nous . . ."
55. Got off track
58. "There you are!"
59. 1967 Pulitzer poet
62. Sign of healing
63. Kind of jet
64. "___ say more?"
65. In this place
66. Test venues
67. Supplemented
68. Jekyll's counterpart

DOWN

1. Dingus
2. Sock pattern
3. "Get with it!"
4. Atlanta-to-Tampa dir.
5. California peninsula
6. Western Indians
7. Energy for Fulton
8. Decline
9. Leafy shelter
10. Discounted
11. Scrooge's cry
12. Yes, at the altar
13. Dupe
19. "Terrible" czar
21. One of the financial markets, for short
23. Bog
25. Hwy. eatery
26. A or B, on a cassette
27. Literary monogram
29. "___ helpless as a kitten up a tree . . ."
30. Dial sound
33. Vitamin bottle abbr.
34. Actress Ward
35. Once, once
37. Florentine river
38. "Le Roi d'Ys" composer
39. Stacked
40. ___ even keel
41. Brief time
44. Trees with catkins
45. Italian refreshments
47. English travel writer Thomas
48. Founder of est
49. U.S. Navy builder
51. Stadium
52. Levied
53. Located
56. Locale of riches
57. Oklahoma city
59. Whole shebang
60. Teachers' org.
61. Collar
62. "No whispering!"

1

G	A	R	B	O		B	A	Y	E	D		N	O	W
A	L	I	E	N		O	L	I	V	E		A	V	A
T	A	B	L	E	H	O	P	P	E	R		M	I	X
			G	N	A	T	S		N	I	C	E	N	E
S	A	T	I	E	T	Y		D	I	V	I	D	E	D
C	R	E	A	S	E		L	I	N	E	A	R		
O	M	E	N	S		T	A	N	G	S		O	R	T
L	O	N	S		S	I	Z	E	S		E	P	E	E
D	R	Y		C	O	M	E	R		E	X	P	O	S
	B	L	A	M	E	D		F	A	C	E	I	T	
C	R	O	O	N	E	R		M	I	S	E	R	L	Y
R	I	P	S	A	W		T	A	S	E	R			
A	S	P		S	H	O	W	S	T	O	P	P	E	R
V	E	E		T	A	P	E	S		U	T	T	E	R
E	R	R		A	T	S	E	A		T	S	A	R	S

2

S	A	H	L		D	I	N	G		S	C	A	B	S
O	L	E	O		O	R	E	O		C	A	R	A	T
B	L	A	C	K	J	A	C	K		A	L	I	N	E
		T	O	R	O		K	A	R	L		S	T	E
A	S	H		I	S	H		R	E	D	H	E	A	D
P	A	R	I	S		O	A	T	S		I	S	M	S
B	O	O	M	T	O	W	N		P	E	T			
	W	H	I	T	E	K	N	I	G	H	T			
		O	N	E		H	U	N	G	E	R	E	D	
I	C	B	M		L	O	S	T		E	R	A	T	O
B	L	U	E	F	L	U		S	O	D		C	A	T
I	A	N		I	O	T	A		N	O	A	H		
S	I	G	M	A		G	R	E	E	N	B	E	A	N
E	R	E	C	T		U	L	N	A		B	A	L	I
S	E	E	M	S		N	O	E	L		A	L	I	T

3

C	H	E	R		D	E	B	T		D	R	U	G	S
L	A	L	O		I	T	E	R		E	E	R	I	E
O	L	I	N		V	A	L	E		P	A	I	N	T
G	O	O	D	W	I	L	L	S	H	O	P			
	S	T	O	O	D		I	S	I	S		A	R	I
		S	V	E	N		M	E	R	L	I	N		
O	P	S		E	N	A	C	T		A	I	D	A	
F	R	I	E	N	D	S	H	I	P	S	E	V	E	N
F	O	N	T		T	I	T	L	E		E	R	E	
E	X	C	E	S	S		O	A	R	S				
R	Y	E		H	E	I	R		T	I	L	E	D	
		P	E	A	C	E	O	F	F	I	C	E	R	
A	C	A	R	E		I	N	D	O		C	O	L	E
S	I	M	O	N		N	E	E	R		E	L	L	E
H	A	I	F	A		G	E	R	M		R	E	A	D

4

B	I	T	E		M	A	T	A		C	L	U	E	D
A	Q	U	A		A	M	O	R		L	A	N	A	I
A	S	T	R	O	K	E	O	F	G	E	N	I	U	S
				R	I	N	K		R	A	G			
O	L	D	H	A	N	D		P	O	V	E	R	T	Y
B	E	R	I	N	G		F	A	C	E		E	E	E
S	T	I	N	G		N	O	D	E		R	T	E	S
	I	F	E	E	L	Y	O	U	R	P	A	I	N	
O	T	T	S		E	L	L	A		U	N	T	I	E
O	B	E		L	A	O	S		S	T	O	L	E	N
H	E	R	M	A	N	N		M	O	O	N	E	R	S
			E	S	T		S	E	L	F				
T	H	A	T	T	O	U	C	H	O	F	M	I	N	K
N	I	G	E	L		M	A	T	E		A	C	R	E
T	E	A	R	Y		A	T	A	D		S	H	A	Y

5

M	E	S	S		S	C	A	L	P		S	H	A	M
O	T	T	O		T	A	B	O	O		T	A	X	I
C	H	I	C	K	E	N	O	U	T		U	Z	I	S
K	E	N		A	R	T	Y		A	R	N	E	S	S
S	L	E	A	Z	E			T	O	T				
			G	O	O	S	E	G	O	S	S	A	G	E
R	A	D	I	O		W	A	R	E	S		J	A	Y
E	B	A	N		D	I	V	A	S		D	A	Z	E
N	O	R		L	I	N	E	N		H	I	R	E	D
D	U	C	K	I	N	G	S	T	O	O	L			
			A	R	E			T	O	L	L	E	D	
C	A	C	H	E	T		E	S	T	E		A	V	A
A	L	O	U		T	U	R	K	E	Y	T	R	O	T
I	M	I	N		E	G	G	A	R		N	U	K	E
N	A	N	A		S	H	O	T	S		T	E	E	D

6

```
B R A C E █ I S I S █ S C A M
A E R O S █ N O T E █ H A L E
O N T O P O F T H E W O R L D
B A I L █ P A T E █ A R I A █
A T E █ A T N O █ E V E L Y N
B A S E H I T █ I C Y █ L I U
█ █ L E M █ A R C █ W O N T █
█ S U M M I T M E E T I N G █
O H N O █ S I T █ N I L █ █ █
P O D █ C T S █ S T R E A M S
S W E L L S █ G O R E █ M A T
█ T R E E █ T A V I █ U P T O
T I P O F T H E I C E B E R G
I'M I N █ H O L E █ L E R O I
N E N E █ O U S T █ I R E N E
```

7

```
R I O T █ S M O G █ C A F E S
O S H A █ P I M A █ A D O R E
S N I T █ A R N O █ M A R N E
H O O T E R V I L L E █ T I M
█ █ █ O A T █ S C R I B E S █
D E C O R A T E █ D A D A █ █
A P O █ S N E L L █ S A X O N
M I C H █ S A G A S █ S T L O
S C O O P █ L A M P S █ E D S
█ A L E S █ R E H E A R S E █
A L B E R T A █ A L L █ █ █ █
D I E █ S P R I N G F I E L D
A L A M O █ I T O N █ E T U I
M A C O N █ E C R U █ N C A A
S C H W A █ S H A M █ S H U N
```

8

```
S P C A █ H E L I █ A S S E T
K A H N █ O X E N █ N E A T O
E G A D █ R I T A █ D E L T A
T O N Y O R L A N D O █ B A D
C D E █ D I E T █ I R M A █ █
H A L F O F █ S T R A N G E █
█ █ A R I S T A █ A R D E N █
P A C T █ C A N D O █ G O O D
S T O I C █ S T A B L E █ █ █
C O M M U T E █ D E S P O T █
█ █ M A R E █ A G U A █ E L O
D N A █ S A N F E R N A N D O
R O N D O █ O O N A █ S C A T
A N D O R █ S U I T █ T I G E
B O O T Y █ E L I E █ I L E D
```

9

```
A S C A P █ M I D A S █ F T C
R O O N E █ A D O L L █ O R O
C H A T T A N O O G A █ R I B
H O T O R C O L D █ M E T E R
█ █ █ N E E R █ O D E S S A █
V I G I L S █ S U N U N U █ █
A R E A █ M O R O N █ M S G
L I T █ A S A L A R K █ T O E
E S T █ L O C A L █ S E A M █
█ █ Y E L L E R █ S C A R P S
P A S T E D █ █ P E R M █ █ █
A M B O Y █ E M O T I O N A L
L O U █ C H I C K A M A U G A
E U R █ A E R I E █ E N N U I
O R G █ T H E I R █ A S S A D
```

10

```
C O M A S █ A K A █ A T T A R
A V A N T █ R O B █ S H O V E
T E D D Y █ C R O S S E Y E D
S N A R L █ H E A L T H █ █ █
█ █ B E E █ W A R Y █ A J A R
S C O W █ L A N D █ G O R E █
T A U █ J A Y S █ A D U L T S
E N T R A P S █ S T E E L I E
P A Y E R S █ Z I N C █ Y E T
I D O S █ L E G O █ E R R S █
N A U T █ S O P H █ P R O █ █
█ █ A L I G H T █ R O G E T █
H A P P Y D A Y S █ A D E L E
E X I L E █ N R A █ T E R S E
P E T E S █ S S W █ E S S E N
```

11

A	H	E	M	■	S	W	O	R	D	■	G	E	N	A
N	O	V	A	■	P	A	T	T	I	■	U	P	O	N
T	W	I	N	C	I	T	I	E	S	■	N	E	E	D
E	L	L	I	O	T	T	S	■	S	A	G	E	L	Y
■	■	F	E	E	■	■	G	O	S	H	■	■	■	■
■	H	O	O	D	■	F	U	L	L	H	O	U	S	E
S	A	U	L	S	■	O	L	I	V	E	■	N	A	G
H	I	N	D	■	D	O	N	N	E	■	D	I	V	A
A	K	C	■	G	E	T	A	T	■	M	E	T	E	D
Q	U	E	E	N	B	E	E	S	■	I	C	E	D	■
■	■	L	A	U	D	■	■	A	N	A	■	■	■	■
D	I	S	O	W	N	■	S	O	R	E	N	E	S	S
A	S	A	P	■	K	I	N	G	C	O	T	T	O	N
Z	A	N	E	■	E	M	I	L	E	■	E	R	M	A
E	Y	E	D	■	D	A	T	E	D	■	D	E	E	P

12

I	A	G	O	■	M	E	S	A	S	■	C	L	U	E
S	H	U	N	■	A	M	I	S	H	■	O	A	T	S
M	A	R	E	■	N	O	L	I	E	■	U	S	E	S
■	B	U	C	K	E	T	O	F	B	O	L	T	S	■
■	■	■	A	N	T	E	■	■	A	R	E	■	■	■
A	D	O	R	E	■	D	O	E	■	B	E	A	D	S
B	E	F	A	L	L	■	F	B	I	■	■	W	E	E
B	A	T	T	L	E	O	F	B	R	I	T	A	I	N
E	R	E	■	■	T	S	E	■	E	N	R	I	C	O
S	Y	N	O	D	■	U	R	N	■	T	A	T	E	R
■	■	■	R	E	S	■	■	U	T	E	P	■	■	■
■	B	E	A	S	T	O	F	B	U	R	D	E	N	■
C	O	I	N	■	A	V	O	I	D	■	O	D	I	N
B	O	R	G	■	G	A	L	L	O	■	O	G	L	E
S	K	E	E	■	E	L	D	E	R	■	R	E	E	D

13

J	A	N	E	■	B	O	T	C	H	■	G	L	A	D
A	B	O	Y	■	E	A	R	L	Y	■	R	E	B	A
B	L	U	E	P	E	R	I	O	D	■	I	V	A	N
S	E	N	S	O	R	■	C	U	E	S	T	I	C	K
■	■	■	S	Y	N	O	D	■	O	S	S	I	E	■
B	E	S	E	T	■	O	L	S	E	N	■	■	■	■
O	C	H	S	■	A	N	O	■	B	A	L	K	E	D
W	H	I	T	E	F	O	R	D	B	R	O	N	C	O
L	O	V	E	L	L	■	H	A	S	■	B	O	R	G
■	■	L	Y	S	O	L	■	N	E	X	U	S	■	■
S	H	A	P	E	■	A	L	I	C	E	■	■	■	■
P	A	G	A	N	I	N	I	■	R	U	G	G	E	D
A	L	A	I	■	R	E	D	H	O	T	M	A	M	A
N	E	I	N	■	I	S	A	A	C	■	A	R	M	Y
S	Y	N	E	■	S	T	Y	L	E	■	C	P	A	S

14

M	A	R	Y	■	S	P	A	T	E	■	D	D	A	Y
E	Z	I	O	■	C	O	M	E	S	■	R	U	L	E
L	U	N	G	■	A	T	O	N	E	■	F	E	T	A
D	R	K	I	L	D	A	R	E	■	P	E	T	E	R
■	■	■	E	S	T	■	M	E	T	E	O	R	S	■
P	A	N	D	A	■	O	N	E	I	L	L	■	■	■
L	E	A	R	N	S	■	E	N	D	■	G	A	S	H
A	R	I	D	■	H	A	R	T	E	■	O	L	E	O
N	O	L	O	■	R	I	V	■	R	H	O	D	E	S
■	■	L	A	U	R	E	L	■	A	D	A	P	T	■
S	Y	R	I	N	G	E	■	I	S	R	■	■	■	■
M	E	A	T	Y	■	D	R	Z	H	I	V	A	G	O
I	S	I	T	■	M	A	I	Z	E	■	O	U	R	S
T	E	L	L	■	A	L	L	I	E	■	I	T	A	L
E	S	S	E	■	H	E	L	E	N	■	D	O	D	O

15

R	U	L	E	D	■	S	H	O	P	■	S	H	A	G
E	P	O	X	Y	■	C	O	L	A	■	T	A	R	A
E	L	O	P	E	■	A	B	E	L	■	A	R	I	Z
L	I	F	O	■	B	R	O	O	M	H	I	L	D	A
S	T	A	N	L	E	Y	■	■	E	I	R	E	■	■
■	■	E	E	G	■	B	E	T	S	■	Q	U	A	■
S	H	A	N	A	■	A	I	N	T	■	S	U	N	S
M	O	P	T	H	E	F	L	O	O	R	W	I	T	H
U	M	P	S	■	N	A	G	S	■	C	A	N	O	E
G	E	L	■	Y	O	R	E	■	A	P	T	■	■	■
■	■	I	G	O	R	■	■	S	U	T	T	E	R	S
V	A	C	U	U	M	P	A	C	K	■	E	R	I	E
E	R	A	S	■	I	O	T	A	■	R	A	N	D	D
R	E	N	T	■	T	R	O	D	■	O	M	E	G	A
B	A	T	S	■	Y	E	P	S	■	E	S	S	E	N

16

17

18

19

20

21

B	A	C	H		S	T	R	A	W		A	P	S	E
A	C	R	E		C	A	I	R	O		S	E	A	L
T	H	E	M	A	R	X	B	R	O	T	H	E	R	S
S	E	W		G	E	E	S				A	E	R	I	E
			L	E	A	D		M	E	T	S			
T	A	O	I	S	M		D	I	R	T		G	A	S
A	I	R	S		F	O	L	I	O		R	U	T	
S	L	A	P	S	T	I	C	K	C	O	M	E	D	Y
T	E	T		P	A	R	K	S			A	B	E	L
E	Y	E		L	I	E	S		S	E	R	E	N	E
		B	A	L	D		R	U	N	S				
I	S	L	E	S		W	E	L	D		U	B	I	
T	H	E	T	H	R	E	E	S	T	O	O	G	E	S
C	O	A	T		E	M	B	E	R		F	L	E	E
H	O	P	E		D	U	S	T	Y		T	Y	P	E

22

A	M	A	S		P	S	A	T		G	A	U	N	T
L	U	F	T		I	N	G	E		A	N	N	I	E
A	C	R	O		E	O	N	S		U	N	I	T	E
S	H	O	W	E	R	W	I	T	H	L	O	V	E	
			D	R	Y			A	L	Y				
G	A	R	A	G	E		B	R	I	E		K	A	T
A	L	I	C	E		T	O	O	T		A	E	R	O
P	I	P	E	D	O	W	N	W	I	L	L	Y	O	U
E	V	E	S		G	I	G	S		A	L	I	S	T
D	E	N		E	R	G	O		S	P	I	N	E	S
			U	S	E			G	U	S				
	S	I	N	K	S	T	O	A	N	E	W	L	O	W
V	I	N	C	I		E	N	I	D		A	U	R	A
I	L	I	U	M		E	T	N	A		R	A	C	Y
M	O	T	T	O		N	O	S	Y		D	U	H	S

23

S	I	F	T		L	A	T	I	N		B	A	B	E
H	O	L	E		A	B	A	C	I		A	W	O	L
A	T	O	M		M	Y	M	A	N		S	L	A	M
H	A	P	P	Y	A	S	A	L	A	R	K			
			I	R	S			R	E	A	M	S		
E	A	S	T	E	R		C	H	E	S	T	N	U	T
M	E	T	A	L		A	H	O	Y			N	S	A
P	R	O	U	D	A	S	A	P	E	A	C	O	C	K
I	I	I		D	O	P	E		G	A	Y	L	E	
R	A	C	C	O	O	N	S		T	E	N	S	E	S
E	L	S	I	E			B	A	N					
		C	R	A	Z	Y	A	S	A	L	O	O	N	
N	O	N	E		R	O	O	S	T		A	B	L	E
O	D	O	R		A	L	L	I	E		S	O	D	A
R	E	D	O		B	A	K	E	R		T	E	S	T

24

S	L	A	P		L	A	M	A		N	A	C	H	O
A	E	R	O		I	D	Y	L		A	G	A	I	N
R	A	M	P		S	A	C	K		Z	E	S	T	A
G	R	E	A	T	P	Y	R	A	M	I	D	S		
E	N	T	R	Y			O	L	D			A	D	A
			T	R	A	F	F	I	C	C	O	N	E	S
S	H	H		N	E	T			A	D	D	I	S	
H	A	Y	R	I	D	E		F	A	B	E	R	G	E
A	D	D	E	R			A	L	P			A	N	S
P	E	R	F	E	C	T	C	U	B	E	S			
E	S	O		A	I	R			R	A	M	B	O	
		F	O	U	R	C	Y	L	I	N	D	E	R	S
I	C	O	N	S		K	L	A	N		D	E	E	S
C	R	I	M	E		L	I	S	T		A	S	T	I
H	O	L	E	S		E	C	H	O		M	E	T	E

25

G	I	B	B	S		E	B	B		B	O	F	F	O
A	D	E	L	A		R	I	A		E	N	L	A	I
B	O	G	A	R	T	A	N	D	B	A	C	A	L	L
L	L	A	M	A	S			G	A	T	E	W	A	Y
E	S	T	E		O	M	B	E	R					
				N	O	I	R		M	A	A	M	S	
S	A	L	I	N	G	E	R		R	O	B	B	I	E
T	R	A	C	Y	A	N	D	H	E	P	B	U	R	N
A	C	C	E	S	S		D	E	F	E	A	T	E	D
T	H	E	S	E		B	O	I	L					
				E	A	G	L	E		L	O	O	M	
E	S	T	E	V	E	Z		C	L	A	I	R	E	
B	U	R	T	O	N	A	N	D	T	A	Y	L	O	R
A	M	A	T	I		A	I	D		T	E	E	N	Y
N	O	P	A	R		R	T	E		E	R	R	O	L

26

S	C	T	V		B	A	A	L		S	C	R	E	W
A	L	O	E		E	M	M	A		C	L	A	R	O
S	E	L	L		F	O	O	T		A	A	R	O	N
H	O	L	D	Y	O	U	R	H	O	R	S	E	S	
			T	U	R	N			P	E	P			
F	A	A		M	E	T	E	R	E	D		B	A	H
A	B	R	A	M			A	I	R		A	L	I	A
M	I	N	D	Y	O	U	R	M	A	N	N	E	R	S
E	D	I	E		V	A	N			I	N	S	E	T
D	E	E		C	A	R	S	E	A	T		S	S	E
			O	R	R			A	C	R	E			
	B	I	T	E	Y	O	U	R	T	O	N	G	U	E
S	A	N	T	A		A	R	L	O		T	A	S	S
O	C	T	E	T		T	S	A	R		E	V	E	S
S	H	O	R	E		S	A	P	S		R	E	D	O

27

I	C	E	S		S	M	E	L	L		E	P	I	C
S	I	N	E		T	A	B	O	O		X	E	N	A
A	V	E	R		R	A	B	B	I	T	E	A	R	S
A	I	R	F	R	A	M	E		S	E	C	R	E	T
C	L	O	S	E	T		D	A	L	E	S			
			H	A	H		R	A	N		W	E	T	
P	L	A	Z	A		E	D	E	N		J	I	V	E
H	A	R	E	B	R	A	I	N	E	D	I	D	E	A
I	V	A	N		E	R	M	A		O	M	E	N	S
L	A	B		I	Q	S		S	C	I				
			K	N	U	T	E		A	N	N	U	A	L
U	P	S	I	D	E		L	A	R	G	E	S	S	E
B	U	N	N	Y	S	L	O	P	E		R	A	T	E
E	R	I	K		T	Y	P	E	S		V	I	E	D
R	E	P	S		S	E	E	D	S		E	R	R	S

28

G	O	S	H		C	O	M	F	Y		D	A	T	E
O	B	E	Y		A	M	O	R	E		U	R	A	L
L	O	W	E		B	I	T	E	S		A	I	L	S
D	E	N	N	I	S	T	H	E	M	E	N	A	C	E
			A	N	T			A	X	E				
H	A	S		G	A	R	M	E	N	T		A	R	T
A	C	C	T		N	E	R	D		R	E	F	E	R
T	H	E	A	D	D	A	M	S	F	A	M	I	L	Y
C	O	N	D	O		D	O	E	R		T	R	A	M
H	O	T		G	R	E	M	L	I	N		E	Y	E
			T	I	E			S	E	C				
L	E	A	V	E	I	T	T	O	B	E	A	V	E	R
O	P	U	S		G	O	A	P	E		J	I	V	E
S	I	T	E		N	O	T	R	E		U	S	E	D
S	C	O	T		S	L	A	Y	S		N	E	R	O

29

C	A	R	G	O		S	P	A	S		R	I	T	Z
A	L	I	E	N		M	O	R	N		A	R	I	A
S	A	O	N	E		U	O	M	O		H	E	M	P
S	I	T	T	I	N	G	R	O	O	M	S			
			S	L	A	G		R	T	E		P	O	T
P	O	S		L	O	L	A		S	C	R	A	P	E
A	C	T	A		M	I	L	T		C	A	R	P	E
S	T	A	N	D	I	N	G	O	V	A	T	I	O	N
C	A	R	N	E		G	A	M	A		S	A	S	S
A	N	V	I	L	S		E	A	R	N		H	E	Y
L	E	E		L	A	S		R	I	O	S			
			W	A	L	K	I	N	G	S	T	I	C	K
J	U	N	E		T	A	R	O		H	E	N	R	I
A	S	I	A		E	T	A	L		E	A	R	E	D
Y	A	N	K		D	E	E	D		S	L	E	W	S

30

O	P	A	L		P	A	L	E	D		S	A	S	E
S	E	M	I		A	M	O	U	R		C	Z	A	R
S	N	O	B		T	I	A	R	A		R	U	N	G
	D	I	R	T	I	S	N	O	T	D	I	R	T	
			E	R	O	S			E	P	E	E		
A	M	I	T	Y		L	E	G	I	T				
L	O	O	T		U	N	I	T	E	S		E	G	G
B	U	T	O	N	L	Y	M	A	T	T	E	R	I	N
S	E	A		O	N	E	A	L	S		A	I	D	A
			C	H	A	T	S			A	S	K	E	W
	E	C	H	O				O	I	L	Y			
	T	H	E	W	R	O	N	G	P	L	A	C	E	
S	H	O	W		O	H	A	R	A		C	O	Z	Y
T	O	R	E		T	O	M	E	S		E	L	I	A
U	S	E	D		C	H	E	S	S		S	T	O	P

31

```
G A I T     B R I E     R O M P
A D L I B   L O L L     O V A L
G O L D I L O C K S     S E R E
      B L I N K     I B E R I A
D E F I L E D     K N O B B E D
E M O T E D     B R O G U E
F I R S T   H E A R     D A T E
A L B     S C O F F E D     R I D
T E E S     O M I T   A G I N G
      A V O C E T     G R U N G E
S T R E A K S     T A N A G E R
C H A L K S     A R L E N
R A N T     U N B E A R A B L E
O N C E     R U E S     S C I O N
D E E R     E N D S     O N U S
```

32

NABS · LEHAR · TLC
ARLO · OXEYE · SHEA
STANDUPANDCHEER
ASH · RIOT · OUTRE
· BASS · PARLAYS
ENRAGE · SAUNA
LAIR · STYLE · ABE
SITBACKANDRELAX
ALE · PLATE · GALE
· ROUTE · SPORES
PAROLEE · DUOS
IDEAL · GOBS · AHA
LIEDOWNONTHEJOB
LESS · ABDUL · NAPE
SUE · CASTE · EXIT

33

TEMP · FADS · CLAD
ARCO · IRAE · BRINY
JAIL · LAZE · LUNGE
· LATTERLADDER
ASSUME · IDEALS
WETTERWEDDER
ALIEN · HEEDS · PAN
KENS · DIRTY · RAMA
EST · BASIE · CYNIC
· BITTERBIDDER
ALSACE · ATEASE
MUTTERMUDDER
ALOOP · IBID · CURD
NUNNS · SEMI · USER
ASES · TREE · PAVE

34

UNCLE · DEER · EVAN
SOLAR · RAKE · MINE
AMOUR · ORES · USER
FEUD · WONDERLAND
· DECAL · TOASTS
CONRAD · BESOT
UNI · DICED · TESLA
EONS · SALEM · SHOW
DREAR · FINAL · ABE
· LEVEE · YAWNED
REGALE · SOBIG
IVORYTOWER · ERSE
PARI · OSHA · ALIEN
EDGE · ELAL · IDLED
NEED · DOTS · TSARS

35

HAGAR · DRAW · BLUR
ALICE · EASE · LANE
ILLTHINKABOUTIT
· SENSE · RECTI
ALP · AGE · BANSHEE
RELATE · CARET
OVAL · BALER · SAG
MAYBEYESMAYBENO
ARS · LAITY · ARGO
· PAWNS · RUGGED
SHARING · AYN · ELS
LENIN · TRACT
ASKMEAGAINLATER
ISLE · CARS · OCALA
NEER · HYPE · GOTIT

36

B	A	K	U		E	T	T	A		F	A	C	E	S
A	S	I	N		L	A	W	S		I	N	A	N	E
S	T	E	T		E	R	I	C		N	A	V	E	L
H	A	V	I	N	G	A	G	O	O	D	T	I	M	E
			L	A	I			T	K	O		L	Y	S
U	M	P		P	A	S	T		R	U	T			
P	E	R	F	E	C	T	W	E	A	T	H	E	R	
I	G	O	R			E	E	L			I	V	A	N
	A	W	E	S	O	M	E	S	C	E	N	E	R	Y
		E	T	H		D	E	A	L		N	E	E	
T	W	A		A	I	R			B	I	G			
W	I	S	H	Y	O	U	W	E	R	E	H	E	R	E
A	S	T	O	P		D	A	L	I		O	D	O	R
N	E	H	R	U		E	G	A	D		S	N	A	G
G	R	E	A	T		R	E	N	E		T	A	R	O

37

G	I	L	T		T	O	R	A	H		I	H	O	P
I	G	O	R		A	R	O	M	A		N	O	N	O
B	A	T	E	S	M	O	T	E	L		S	L	I	T
E	S	T	A	T	E			S	T	R	A	I	T	S
			S	U	R	G	E		S	A	N	D		
A	R	G	O	N		A	N	T		T	E	A	S	E
W	O	R	N		A	R	T	I	S	T		Y	O	M
A	D	A		B	L	A	R	N	E	Y		I	D	O
R	E	N		L	E	G	A	T	E		G	N	A	T
D	O	D	G	E		E	N	E		S	E	N	S	E
			H	E	E	L		T	R	A	P	S		
B	L	O	N	D	I	E			T	A	T	T	E	R
M	I	T	T		P	L	A	Z	A	S	U	I	T	E
O	R	E	L		I	M	P	E	L		R	E	N	D
C	A	L	E		D	O	O	N	E		E	R	A	S

38

G	E	N	O	A		I	S	N	T		S	W	I	M
O	V	E	N	S		S	T	A	R		O	H	N	O
R	E	A	C	H	E	S	A	V	E	R	D	I	C	T
A	N	T	E		P	U	N	Y		O	A	T	H	S
N	T	H		L	I	E	D		E	A	S	E		
			T	E	C		S	H	A	M		S	O	N
O	R	I	O	N		A	C	E	S		D	A	M	E
L	O	N	G	A	R	M	O	F	T	H	E	L	A	W
E	L	S	A		A	I	N	T		E	B	E	R	T
G	E	T		K	I	E	V		T	N	T			
		E	D	E	N		I	O	U	S		B	A	N
S	T	A	R	R		I	C	O	N		B	R	I	O
O	R	D	E	R	I	N	T	H	E	C	O	U	R	T
L	E	O	S		A	L	E	E		I	N	N	E	R
D	E	F	S		M	A	D	D		A	N	O	D	E

39

A	T	O	M		F	O	R	M	S		N	A	S	A
D	I	V	E		E	L	I	S	E		I	N	O	N
D	R	A	W	B	R	I	D	G	E	A	H	E	A	D
S	O	L		L	A	V	E		D	M	I	T	R	I
			C	O	L	E		U	T	I	L			
A	P	A	R	T		S	A	T	I	N		G	O	B
S	E	T	A	T			S	A	M		I	R	A	E
K	E	E	P	O	F	F	T	H	E	G	R	A	S	S
E	L	I	S		I	L	E			R	A	D	I	O
D	E	N		E	V	E	R	S		A	T	E	S	T
			S	T	E	W		H	O	T	E			
S	E	D	A	N	S		B	I	T	E		G	A	L
P	R	I	V	A	T	E	E	N	T	R	A	N	C	E
E	I	N	E		A	G	A	T	E		M	A	M	A
D	E	A	R		R	O	T	O	R			S	T	E	P

40

R	B	I	S		C	O	L	O	N		R	O	M	A
A	L	O	E		O	R	A	T	E		U	K	E	S
P	U	N	C	T	U	A	T	I	O	N	M	A	R	K
	E	S	T	O	P			S	N	A	P	P	L	E
			M	E	T	S		S	L	I	E	R		
L	I	C	I	T		I	N	V	I	T	E			
O	R	O	N	O		N	E	E	R			P	I	P
P	A	N	A	M	A	C	A	N	A	L	C	I	T	Y
E	N	E		S	A	K	I		E	A	S	E	L	
			I	R	E	N	I	C		A	W	A	R	E
A	E	T	N	A			N	E	I	N				
T	R	O	T	T	E	D		S	T	E	A	K		
I	N	T	E	S	T	I	N	A	L	O	R	G	A	N
L	I	E	N		A	N	O	D	E		G	O	R	E
T	E	S	T		L	O	R	D	S		O	G	L	E

41

C	A	M	A	Y		A	L	E	U	T		M	A	R
O	H	A	R	E		B	I	L	K	O		I	C	E
P	A	N	T	S	P	O	C	K	E	T		S	H	A
			D	A	R	K			E	N	S	O	R	
D	I	L	B	E	R	T		J	I	B	B	O	O	M
U	V	U	L	A	S		B	A	T	A	A	N		
P	A	C	E	R		S	O	B	I	G		E	F	T
E	N	I	D		G	L	O	B	S		T	S	A	R
S	A	L		L	L	A	M	A		T	A	C	K	Y
	L	A	Y	U	P	S		V	E	N	U	E	S	
P	R	E	L	I	M	S		D	E	S	S	E	R	T
R	A	B	I	N			A	I	N	T				
O	V	A		G	I	M	M	E	A	B	R	E	A	K
B	E	L		T	R	A	I	T		A	D	D	L	E
E	L	L		O	K	I	E	S		N	A	T	T	Y

42

S	I	L	O		B	A	L	S	A		S	H	O	P
O	R	A	L		A	S	I	A	N		P	A	N	E
H	A	N	D	I	N	H	A	N	D		O	R	C	A
O	N	E		S	T	E	M		E	M	O	T	E	R
			A	L	E	S		C	R	A	F	T		
A	M	B	L	E	R		L	O	S	T	S	O	U	L
D	E	L	I	S		C	A	N	O	E		H	B	O
A	L	O	T		R	O	U	E	N		G	A	O	L
M	E	W		B	E	R	R	Y		C	O	R	A	L
N	E	B	R	A	S	K	A		C	H	A	T	T	Y
			Y	O	K	E	S		F	O	A	L		
E	M	B	L	E	M		A	L	L	I		S	O	B
V	I	L	A		B	L	U	E	O	N	B	L	U	E
I	R	O	N		L	A	D	E	N		I	O	T	A
L	E	W	D		E	D	I	T	S		T	E	S	T

43

S	A	Y	S		A	W	A	C	S		A	R	I	D
U	T	A	H		Z	E	B	R	A		S	O	R	E
E	A	S	Y	S	T	R	E	E	T		S	C	A	N
T	R	I	N	I		E	T	T	A		U	K	E	S
	I	R	E	N	E		S	E	N	T	R	Y		
		S	E	A	M				H	E	R	B	S	
R	A	H	S		G	A	R	A	G	E		O	A	K
U	S	A		M	A	H	A	T	M	A		A	L	I
M	I	R		E	N	I	G	M	A		O	D	D	S
S	A	D	A	T			S	T	I	R				
		D	R	A	M	A	S		S	M	A	S	H	
H	A	R	I		A	L	A	W		O	C	C	U	R
A	S	I	S		N	A	T	H	A	N	L	A	N	E
H	A	V	E		I	N	E	E	D		E	L	A	N
A	P	E	S		C	A	S	T	S		S	E	N	D

44

C	U	B	E		S	L	A	S	H		P	I	P	E
A	P	E	X		M	A	I	N	E		O	V	I	D
P	O	R	T	L	A	N	D	O	R		C	A	N	I
E	N	G		U	R	G	E		O	R	A	N	G	E
			A	R	T	E		I	C	E	T			
S	M	I	L	E	Y		P	R	O	C	E	S	S	
W	I	L	L	S		G	O	O	P		L	E	M	A
A	L	O	E		N	O	O	N	S		L	O	A	N
T	E	N	N		O	N	L	Y		C	O	U	L	D
	R	A	T	I	N	G	S		R	E	I	L	L	Y
			O	N	U	S		W	A	R	D			
A	V	O	W	E	R		A	A	R	E		W	O	E
N	E	O	N		B	E	T	H	E	S	D	A	M	D
C	A	P	P		A	L	T	O	S		O	R	I	G
E	L	S	A		N	O	N	O	T		A	N	T	E

45

B	A	C	K		B	A	B	U		T	I	M	O	R
A	L	E	E		I	R	I	S		I	M	A	G	E
H	O	L	Y	R	O	M	A	N	E	M	P	I	R	E
N	E	T		O	L	E	S		D	O	O	M	E	D
			B	U	O	Y		B	I	T	S			
	D	O	I	N	G		B	A	C	H	E	L	O	R
M	I	N	G	D	Y	N	A	S	T	Y		U	T	A
O	P	E	D			O	N	S		A	C	T	I	
O	S	T		O	L	D	D	O	M	I	N	I	O	N
G	O	O	D	B	Y	E	S		A	N	T	E	S	
			A	V	I	S		A	R	C	S			
S	I	N	G	I	N		A	S	T	A		E	R	A
T	H	E	M	A	G	I	C	K	I	N	G	D	O	M
A	I	M	A	T		T	H	E	N		B	I	L	E
S	T	O	R	E		S	E	W	S		S	T	Y	X

46

S	A	H	I	B		F	L	A	B		R	O	A	M
E	L	I	S	E		R	O	B	E		O	N	C	E
P	A	P	E	R	T	I	G	E	R		C	E	D	E
A	M	P	E	R	A	G	E		A	C	K	A	C	K
L	O	O		I	I	I		E	T	C	H			
			E	L	D		R	I	C	O	T	T	A	
C	A	N	I	S		P	I	N		U	R	A	L	
O	W	A	R		S	L	A	N	G		N	I	K	E
M	O	T	O		C	A	D		E	D	G	E	S	
B	L	E	N	D	I	N		S	P	A				
		H	O	E	D		T	O	R		O	P	S	
D	I	S	O	W	N		D	A	M	N	A	B	L	E
O	D	O	R		C	L	A	Y	P	I	G	E	O	N
T	E	N	S		E	A	V	E		N	E	S	T	S
S	A	G	E		S	P	E	D		G	E	E	S	E

47

O	F	F	E	R		H	O	P	I		D	O	Z	E
C	R	E	T	E		A	V	O	N		E	M	I	L
H	E	R	E	S		G	E	N	T		V	A	N	S
O	D	D		T	O	U	R	D	E	F	O	R	C	E
		E	C	O	L	E			R	U	T			
M	I	L	O	R	D		G	I	N	S	E	N	G	
I	R	A	T	E		W	A	L	E	S		O	A	S
D	O	N	E		C	A	S	E	D		O	M	I	T
I	N	C		G	R	A	S	S		P	A	D	U	A
	S	E	C	R	E	C	Y		A	R	R	E	S	T
			A	I	D			C	R	I	S	P		
C	O	U	P	D	E	G	R	A	C	E		L	O	T
A	N	N	O		N	O	I	R		S	A	U	T	E
R	E	I	N		Z	E	S	T		T	I	M	O	N
A	R	T	S		A	S	E	A		S	L	E	E	T

48

L	A	R	V	A		D	A	N	G		M	O	P	
E	L	I	O	T		U	S	E	R	S		O	V	A
M	I	N	U	T	E	S	T	E	A	K		P	E	W
		S	A	N	T	A		T	I	G	E	R	S	
S	O	L		C	R	Y		H	E	R	O	D		
T	R	A	S	H	Y		S	O	F	T	B	A	L	L
R	A	M	I	E		M	I	N	U	S		R	A	E
A	C	E	D		P	I	X	E	L		I	O	T	A
I	L	E		B	O	N	E	S		B	R	U	I	N
T	E	X	T	I	L	E	S		G	L	E	N	N	E
		C	A	C	A	O		S	O	U		D	A	R
P	A	U	P	E	R		B	A	S	E	S			
A	M	S		P	O	L	I	S	H	J	O	K	E	S
P	I	E		S	I	E	G	E		A	R	E	A	S
A	D	S			D	A	D	S		Y	E	A	R	N

49

C	L	A	N		H	A	D	J		S	L	A	K	E
O	U	S	E		A	R	I	A		H	I	T	I	T
C	A	S	H	M	E	R	E	S	W	E	A	T	E	R
O	U	T	R	E			S	P	H	E	R	U	L	E
A	S	S	U	R	E	S		E	O	N				
				S	U	P	R	A		T	M	A	N	
E	M	B	A	T	T	L	E		Q	U	I	T	E	
C	H	E	C	K	O	U	T	C	O	U	N	T	E	R
R	O	D	E	O			R	E	P	E	A	T	E	D
U	S	E	D		C	H	I	D	E					
				W	O	O		E	N	I	G	M	A	S
A	P	P	O	I	N	T	S			D	R	A	M	A
C	H	A	R	G	E	D	A	F	F	A	I	R	E	S
D	I	T	C	H		O	A	H	U		D	A	B	S
C	L	E	A	T		G	R	A	M		S	T	A	Y

50

A	L	A	S		A	W	O	L		P	E	A	C	H
P	E	P	E		M	A	K	E		A	C	H	O	O
H	A	R	P		E	L	A	N		C	L	O	M	P
I	V	E	T	O	L	D	Y	O	U	M	A	Y	B	E
D	E	S		M	I	O			N	A	T			
			B	A	A		A	G	I	N		D	U	B
S	A	R	A	N		O	S	L	O		L	I	S	A
T	W	O	M	I	L	L	I	O	N	T	I	M	E	S
U	R	S	A		A	D	A	M		H	E	E	D	S
B	Y	E		E	D	E	N		F	E	D			
			S	M	L			O	U	R		P	A	P
N	O	T	T	O	E	X	A	G	G	E	R	A	T	E
E	L	I	O	T		M	I	L	E		A	C	R	E
C	A	D	R	E		A	D	E	E		V	E	I	L
K	N	E	E	D		S	A	S	S		E	R	A	S

51

B	R	A		S	A	L	E	R	N	O		A	S	H
O	O	P		C	L	O	S	E	U	P		T	A	O
X	C	H	R	O	M	O	S	O	M	E		O	N	A
		O	N	T	A	P		B	R	A	N	D	X	
C	A	R	A	T		E	M	O		A	C	A	R	E
A	L	I			D	I	P	S		C	L	A	D	
M	E	S	S	E	S		S	A	T	I	E			
	X	M	A	R	K	S	T	H	E	S	P	O	T	
		W	R	I	T	E		M	O	T	L	E	Y	
B	U	F	F		T	O	R	N				I	L	E
A	P	R	I	L		A	X	E		M	A	V	E	N
X	R	A	T	E	D			A	M	U	S	E		
T	O	Y		G	E	N	E	R	A	T	I	O	N	X
E	S	E		E	L	E	M	E	N	T		I	N	K
R	E	D		R	E	T	U	R	N	S		L	E	E

52

S	H	A	Q		P	G	A		A	P	S	I	S
N	A	S	A		U	F	O	S		S	E	E	M	E
L	I	S	T		S	C	O	T	C	H	T	A	P	E
	E	A	S	E		F	O	O		E	T	A	L
G	I	N	R	U	M	M	Y		N	O	S	A	L	E
H	A	T		P	E	A		M	A	V		C	A	Y
I	M	T	H	E		L	E	A	N	E	R		
	B	O	U	R	B	O	N	S	T	R	E	E	T
	E	M	E	N	D	S		D	O	T	E	R	
N	B	C		A	N	E		E	M	U		C	R	O
O	I	L	I	N	G		R	Y	E	B	R	E	A	D
T	E	E	S		A	S	A		L	S	A	T	
B	R	A	N	D	Y	W	I	N	E		Z	E	R	O
A	C	T	O	R		A	S	H	E		O	R	E	O
D	E	S	T	E		G	E	L		R	A	M	P

53

C	O	M	P		S	P	R	I	G		S	H	E	D
A	R	E	A		H	O	U	S	E		P	U	M	A
L	I	L	T		A	T	S	E	A		A	C	I	D
L	O	V	E	O	N	T	H	E	R	O	C	K	S	
E	L	I		M	A	S			H	E	S	S	E
R	E	N	T	A		M	A	I	M		T	A	G
	U	N	I	C	O	R	N		A	E	R	O
	A	R	R	I	D	E	X	T	R	A	D	R	Y	
G	R	I	N		A	N	I	S	E	E	D	
O	T	C		E	S	T	E		T	S	A	R	S
V	I	O	L	A			S	E	N		N	E	E
	S	C	A	R	E	D	S	T	R	A	I	G	H	T
B	A	H	S		F	R	I	A	R		M	E	E	T
O	N	E	S		T	A	N	G	O		A	L	A	E
A	S	T	O		S	T	E	E	L		N	A	T	E

54

P	R	I	D	E		T	S	A	R		B	L	A	B
L	O	C	A	L		H	E	R	E		R	U	L	E
A	T	O	N	E		O	V	E	N		A	S	I	A
T	O	N	I	C		R	E	N	O		S	T	A	N
			S	T	P		N	A	I	L	S			
H	I	G	H	R	O	A	D		R	E	H	U	N	G
A	N	A		A	N	G	E	R		T	A	B	O	R
G	O	N	G		G	R	A	I	L		T	O	N	E
A	N	G	L	E		A	D	D	U	P		A	C	E
R	E	S	U	M	E		L	I	N	E	A	T	E	D
			T	U	M	M	Y		A	R	M			
P	S	S	T		M	O	S	S		M	O	N	K	S
E	C	H	O		E	V	I	L		I	R	E	N	E
R	A	I	N		T	I	N	A		T	A	R	O	T
E	N	V	Y		T	E	S	T		S	L	O	T	H

55

P	A	I	R		C	R	A	M		L	A	T	H	E
A	L	D	A		H	E	R	A		E	R	R	O	L
R	E	L	I	G	I	O	U	S	R	I	T	U	A	L
R	E	E	L	I	N		M	A	O		S	E	R	A
			A	G	E	S		D	O	N				
B	R	I	T	I	S	H	S	A	T	I	R	I	S	T
R	A	N		E	A	T		S	P	O	R	T	Y
A	C	T	E	D		M	R	S		S	T	A	R	K
G	E	R	M	A	N		A	L	P		N	E	E
G	R	O	U	P	O	F	W	A	R	S	H	I	P	S
			S	P	A		M	O	U	E				
A	N	K	A		A	W	L		B	R	A	V	O	S
F	I	N	G	E	R	N	A	I	L	F	L	E	S	H
A	L	I	E	N		E	L	S	E		E	R	L	E
R	E	T	R	O		D	O	O	M		R	O	O	S

S	C	A	T		S	H	E	E	N		F	A	K	E
T	A	B	U		T	A	N	G	O		E	V	A	N
A	L	O	T		A	R	I	E	L		L	A	T	E
B	L	U	E	E	Y	E	D	S	O	U	L			
L	I	N	E	N				T	A	F	F	E	T	A
E	N	D		D	I	O	R		D	O	O	D	A	D
		P	O	N	D	E	R			R	E	I	D	
	B	R	O	W	N	E	Y	E	D	G	I	R	L	
S	A	U	L			R	E	P	E	A	T			
A	L	L	I	E	D		S	O	N	Y		I	T	T
D	I	E	T	E	R	S			L	A	M	E	R	
		B	L	A	C	K	E	Y	E	D	P	E	A	
P	E	R	U		P	A	U	L	O		L	A	N	D
A	G	A	R		E	L	D	E	R		E	L	S	E
S	O	H	O		S	P	O	C	K		R	A	Y	S

S	T	A	G		T	A	L	K		B	A	S	S	O
P	A	L	E		E	T	O	N		A	N	N	U	L
A	L	I	T	T	L	E	B	I	R	D	T	O	L	D
R	E	T	I	R	E		S	C	A	M		B	U	S
		T	E	T	E		K	N	O	B				
A	C	T		S	H	A	M		D	U	R	E	S	S
B	R	A	S		O	R	E	M		T	O	N	I	C
Y	O	U	C	A	N	T	D	O	T	H	I	S	T	O
S	O	P	O	R		H	O	P	E		L	U	A	U
S	K	E	T	C	H		C	E	R	T		E	R	R
		S	H	U	T		S	M	U	T				
A	L	L		D	R	A	T		I	N	U	R	E	S
H	E	Y	B	U	T	W	H	A	T	A	B	O	U	T
U	M	I	A	K		N	A	M	E		A	I	R	E
M	A	N	S	E		Y	I	P	S		S	L	O	P

A	L	D	E	R		A	B	B	R		L	E	C	H
Q	U	I	R	E		S	O	R	E		E	L	L	A
U	N	C	A	P		H	O	E	S		A	V	O	W
A	G	E		T	I	C	K	L	E	D	P	I	N	K
		A	I	D	A		R	E	E	S	E	S		
B	U	B	B	L	I	N	G	O	V	E	R			
U	T	I	L	E		E	W	E	R		J	I	B	
R	A	K	E		P	I	N	E	D		Z	A	N	E
R	H	O		L	I	L	I		F	A	V	R	E	
		W	A	L	K	I	N	G	O	N	A	I	R	
V	I	S	A	G	E			A	I	R	Y			
O	N	C	L	O	U	D	N	I	N	E		R	P	M
C	O	A	L		P	A	I	L		V	O	I	L	A
A	N	N	E		O	N	C	E		E	L	L	E	N
L	E	T	T		N	E	E	D		R	E	L	A	X

H	A	N	E	S		F	R	A	T		R	I	M	E
E	Q	U	A	L		R	A	G	A		I	R	A	S
C	U	R	R	Y	F	A	V	O	R		V	A	C	S
K	A	E	L		A	N	I		G	E	N	R	E	
		M	I	N	T	C	O	N	D	I	T	I	O	N
A	L	B	E	E		E	L	O	I	S	E			
L	E	E	R	A	T		I	O	N		R	T	E	S
A	I	R		L	O	T		N	E	T		A	L	E
S	A	G	S		W	A	F		D	A	R	N	I	T
		O	P	E	R	A	S			C	A	G	E	S
B	A	S	I	L	R	A	T	H	B	O	N	E		
E	N	T	R	Y			I	R	R		O	R	A	L
A	G	E	E		S	A	G	E	A	D	V	I	C	E
K	L	E	E		S	C	U	D		D	E	N	T	E
S	O	D	S		T	E	E	S		T	R	E	S	S

E	G	A	D		B	A	W	D		E	D	G	E	R
N	A	P	A		O	M	O	O		N	O	O	S	E
D	R	O	M	E	D	A	R	Y		C	R	A	P	S
S	A	T	E	D		S	O	L	O		D	O	T	
U	G	H		S	T	A	T	U	A	R	Y			
P	E	E	P	E	R	S		H	E	E	H	A	W	
	C	A	L	A	I	S		S	L	E	P	T		
T	E	A	R		M	A	O	R	I		P	R	E	S
S	P	R	I	G		I	A	G	R	E	E			
P	A	Y	S	U	P		T	O	O	R	D	E	R	
	H	A	I	L	M	A	R	Y		I	T	E		
S	P	A		N	C	A	A		C	I	T	E	D	
L	A	R	V	A		T	I	P	P	E	R	A	R	Y
A	N	T	I	C		I	N	T	O		A	R	N	E
Y	E	S	N	O		N	E	A	P		N	Y	E	S

61

P	A	R	R		A	D	A	M		A	P	R	E	S
O	B	I	E		L	O	B	O		I	R	A	T	E
L	I	G	H	T	E	N	U	P		R	E	G	A	N
A	D	I	E	U		T	E	L	E	C	A	S	T	
R	E	D	A	L	E	R	T		O	D	E			
			T	A	K	E	A	L	O	A	D	O	F	F
A	R	M		E	L	L	A		L	E	V	E	E	
J	O	Y	R	I	D	E		P	R	E	S	E	T	S
O	W	N	E	D		A	S	T	O		N	E	T	
B	E	A	G	O	O	D	L	O	S	E	R			
			I	L	L		O	P	E	R	E	T	T	A
C	A	S	C	A	D	E	S		I	F	E	E	L	
A	W	A	I	T		T	H	I	N	K	F	A	S	T
P	R	I	D	E		R	E	N	O		E	S	T	O
T	Y	L	E	R		E	D	A	M		D	E	Y	S

62

L	A	M	B		T	A	G	U	P			S	P	A
O	J	A	I		A	R	E	S	O		D	E	E	P
C	A	T	B	U	R	G	L	A	R		A	E	R	O
O	R	E		R	I	O	T		T	O	R	N	U	P
			H	A	F	T		S	H	U	T			
I	T	S	E	L	F		S	M	O	T	H	E	R	S
S	A	H	L		J	A	I	L		V	E	E	P	
A	X	E	L		M	O	N	T	E		A	L	B	A
A	C	E	S		A	N	K	H		D	E	A	R	
C	O	P	A	P	L	E	A		O	N	E	D	G	E
			N	O	D	S		S	P	U	R			
J	I	G	G	L	E		A	H	E	M		S	S	S
O	B	O	E		M	E	N	I	N	B	L	A	C	K
K	E	E	L		E	V	E	R	T		A	L	A	I
E	T	S		R	E	T	R	O		W	A	R	M	

63

O	Z	O	N	E		C	L	A	P		H	A	S	P
T	I	D	A	L		H	A	R	E		E	L	I	A
H	O	I	S	T		A	S	A	P		A	L	M	S
O	N	E	C	O	U	N	T	R	Y		D	O	I	T
			A	N	N		A	S	A	R	U	L	E	
C	H	A	R		H	A	L	T		D	E	T	E	R
P	O	X		K	A	R	O		S	D	S			
O	N	E	C	O	N	S	T	I	T	U	T	I	O	N
			O	R	D		T	A	R	P		S	R	O
E	C	O	L	E		R	E	N	O		A	M	O	R
M	O	N	D	A	L	E		V	A	T				
B	O	S	S		O	N	E	D	E	S	T	I	N	Y
A	K	I	N		P	E	R	U		P	A	S	E	O
R	I	T	A		E	G	I	S		C	R	A	I	G
K	E	E	P		Z	E	S	T		A	S	Y	L	A

64

S	M	I	T		S	H	A	G		G	A	L	L	O
H	A	S	H		H	A	Z	E		A	V	A	I	L
A	G	A	R		I	R	O	N		L	O	R	N	E
H	I	Y	O	S	I	L	V	E	R	A	W	A	Y	
			T	O	T	E		A	H	A				
	T	O	T	H	E	M	O	O	N	A	L	I	C	E
C	A	R	L	O		S	H	A	D		D	D	S	
O	B	O	E		G	R	I	S	T		E	A	R	S
D	O	N		F	L	U	E			A	C	H	O	O
Y	O	O	H	O	O	M	R	S	B	L	O	O	M	
			O	R	O		T	E	E	N				
	B	E	A	M	M	E	U	P	S	C	O	T	T	Y
D	O	G	G	O		G	P	A	S		M	O	U	E
A	N	A	I	S		E	T	U	I		I	O	N	A
M	E	D	E	A		R	O	L	E		C	L	A	N

65

A	G	E	D		A	M	E	N	S		S	N	I	P
R	O	M	E		M	E	D	I	A		L	O	R	I
O	T	I	C		S	L	I	C	K		O	N	E	S
S	I	L	K	S	T	O	C	K	I	N	G	S		
E	T	E		P	E	N	T		T	A	M	P	S	
			A	I	L	S		S	C	H	N	O	O	K
	E	D	G	E		O	R	O		K	E	Y		
	G	O	O	D	Y	T	W	O	S	H	O	E	S	
E	R	G		U	S	S		A	I	R	Y			
R	E	F	R	A	M	E		H	U	R	L			
S	T	I	E	S		R	E	P	S		B	A	A	
			S	T	U	F	F	E	D	S	H	I	R	T	S
H	O	H	O		L	I	E	G	E		H	A	R	I
O	L	E	O		O	N	S	E	T		A	V	I	A
T	A	S	K		W	E	E	D	S		D	E	A	N

66

```
G O B S . W A D I . L A V E R
A N U T . E B O N . I G A V E
M Y R A . S U R F . B A S I E
E X P R E S S Y O U R S E L F
. . . V E E . B A S . . . .
V E R T E X . F L O . I M A M
O N A I R . G R E A T . E R E
L O C A L A N E S T H E S I A
T R E . Y E A R S . R O T O R
A M S O . R T E . P I N A T A
. . P O I . . A R F . . . .
L I M I T E D E D I T I O N S
O B E A H . O X E N . D R O P
S A N T E . O P E C . E A S E
T R U E R . M O P E . A L E X
```

67

```
M A L L . U T T E R . R O A D
A S I A . S U E D E . E R G O
T H E B R O N X I S U P B U T
H E N I E . T E A R O S E S .
. . A T I C . S L I T . . .
G A S L I G H T . E S T A T E
E S T . N O I R E . E X O D
T H E B A T T E R Y S D O W N
N E E R . S N O U T . N I A
O N L A N D . T S A R I S T S
. . G O E S . E N A S . .
T I E G A M E S . T H R E E
I T S A H E L L U V A T O W N
P E A R . A M A N A . A X E D
S M U T . N A T A L . R Y N E
```

68

```
B O I S . C R A B . P I Q U E
R U N E . H E R A . S P U N K
A T T A . I S U P . A S I D E
W H O L E L O T T A L O V E .
L I T . J E R . I B M . E R A
S T O N E . B O Z O . G R A S
. . A C K . N E D . N E C K
H A L F T I M E R E P O R T S
U N I T . T U T . S E M . .
E T N A . K R O C . R E M I X
D I G . W A D . A D D . I S E
. Q U A R T E R P O U N D E R
G U I L E . R I N G . E A U X
T E N O N . E T U I . M I L E
E D I T S . D A T E . O R T S
```

69

```
T R A P . T E E M . S O M E
S A L I C . O R E O . U B E R
P I G E O N T O E D . M A S S
. M E R C I E S . E G A D S
W E B . K L M . A S O C I A L
E N R O B E . T I T O . A G E
S T A R R . S E L L S . H E X
. E A G L E E Y E D . .
P U P . I R O N Y . N I G H T
I K E . N E T S . T E P E E S
T U R E E N S . M A C . O R K
. L I N D A . M I L K E R S .
R E D S . D U C K L E G G E D
A L O U . E S M E . D O I L Y
P E T E . S E X Y . S A F E
```

70

```
C O P E . O M E N . S Y R U P
U P O N . N A M E . H O U S E
J U N G L E J I M . A S H E R
O S S . E D O . O B V E R S E
. . . B E A R D . L E M . .
S P A R K Y . O B E D I E N T
L O G O S . T O E S . T R I O
A N N A . C O D E S . E M E R
I C E D . O L A N . P S A L M
N E W W O R L D . C H A S S E
. . . A C E . S C R I M . .
P L A Y E R S . E E L . D E F
O U I J A . P E C O S B I L L
P I N O N . E V I L . L O S E
E S T E S . D A L E . T R E E
```

71

P	A	P	A	S		A	C	R	E		G	A	M	A
C	L	A	S	P		F	L	A	X		R	E	A	R
S	I	T	K	A		R	A	M	P		E	R	I	C
	T	H	E	T	R	O	U	B	L	E	W	I	T	H
		D	U	O		S	O	O	T		A	R	E	
E	A	T		L	O	W		D	U	E	L	E	D	
T	H	E	R	A	T	R	A	C	E	I	S			
S	A	T	E		E	M	U		A	I	D	A		
	E	V	E	N	I	F	Y	O	U	W	I	N		
W	A	L	L	O	P		F	O	P		O	P	T	
A	R	A		L	I	S	T		W	I	T			
Y	O	U	R	E	S	T	I	L	L	A	R	A	T	
L	U	R	E		T	E	T	E		T	U	L	I	P
A	S	E	A		L	A	L	O		E	S	T	E	R
Y	E	L	P		E	D	E	N		S	T	O	R	Y

72

P	O	D	S		C	L	O	T		T	I	M	I	D
A	V	O	W		R	I	M	E		O	D	I	L	E
D	A	Z	E		A	N	N	A		N	E	L	L	Y
S	L	E	E	P	Y	T	I	M	E	G	A	L		
			P	R	O				F	U	S	S	E	D
A	D	O		I	N	S	P	I	R	E		T	S	E
D	I	N	G	S		T	E	T	E		E	R	T	E
D	R	E	A	M	D	R	E	A	M	D	R	E	A	M
L	E	T	S		R	O	L	L		A	G	A	T	E
E	C	O		C	O	M	E	S	B	Y		M	E	D
S	T	O	P	U	P			E	A	U				
	M	I	S	T	E	R	S	A	N	D	M	A	N	
S	C	A	N	T		C	O	O	T		D	A	L	I
O	U	N	C	E		H	A	L	E		E	X	E	C
D	R	Y	E	R		O	D	O	R		R	I	C	K

73

M	A	T	S		O	L	G	A		R	E	A	T	A
E	L	A	L		D	U	O	S		E	L	L	I	S
A	G	H	A		D	A	L	I		D	M	A	R	K
N	A	O	M	I	J	U	D	D		H	E	R	E	S
S	E	E	S	T	O		E	D	E	R				
			T	B	A	R		U	N	F	A	I	R	
C	L	A	R	O		P	A	L	E		U	L	N	A
A	E	R	O		D	E	V	I	L		D	A	F	T
S	A	N	G		I	S	E	E		A	D	I	O	S
T	H	E	E	N	D		L	U	B	E				
			R	O	O	T		A	R	A	B	I	A	
S	W	A	M	I		B	I	L	L	Y	B	U	D	D
C	A	M	U	S		I	D	Y	L		A	S	E	A
A	N	O	D	E		L	E	N	A		T	E	S	T
N	E	R	D	S		L	E	N	D		E	S	T	E

74

A	Z	O	R	E	S		S	H	O	W		C	A	L
B	O	D	E	G	A		L	A	M	E		A	R	E
C	O	S	T	A	R		I	V	A	N		R	I	G
		A	N	A	R	M	A	N	D	A	L	E	G	
S	A	K	I		E	E	N			E	A	S	Y	
C	L	A	N	T	O	N		A	L	B	S			
R	I	B		A	M	A	N		A	R	O	M	A	S
A	B	U	S	H	E	L	A	N	D	A	P	E	C	K
P	I	L	E	O	N		H	A	L	S		T	H	U
			R	E	S	T		F	E	S	T	O	O	N
M	O	L	T			E	A	T			R	O	O	K
A	Y	E	A	R	A	N	D	A	D	A	Y			
B	V	D		A	L	P	O		A	V	O	I	D	S
E	E	G		S	L	I	P		N	O	U	G	A	T
L	Y	E		P	A	N	T		A	N	T	O	N	Y

75

D	A	B	S		B	O	S	S	A		O	B	I	S
O	R	E	S		A	T	T	A	R		N	A	D	A
O	G	R	E		J	O	E	Y	B	I	S	H	O	P
D	Y	E		C	A	S	A	N	O	V	A			
A	L	A	M	O			M	O	R	A	L	I	S	T
D	E	L	I	M	I	T			N	E	H	I	S	
			R	E	M	O	R	S	E		O	D	E	
	A	L	E	X	A	N	D	E	R	P	O	P	E	
S	R	A			S	E	A	L	S	I	N			
E	N	L	A	I			A	T	L	A	S	E	S	
C	O	O	L	C	A	T	S			E	N	T	R	E
			D	E	R	A	I	L	E	D		A	H	A
A	N	N	E	S	E	X	T	O	N		S	C	A	B
L	E	A	R		N	E	E	D	I		H	E	R	E
L	A	B	S		A	D	D	E	D		H	Y	D	E